D1105932

ZEN

AND

TONIC

The Countryman Press
A division of W. W. Norton & Company
Independent Publishers Since 1923

ZEN AND TONIC

SAVORY AND FRESH COCKTAILS
for the
ENLIGHTENED DRINKER

JULES ARON

Copyright © 2016 by Julia Aronov
Photographs by Gyorgy Papp

All rights reserved
Printed in China

For information about permission to reproduce selections from this book, write to
Permissions, The Countryman Press, 500 Fifth Avenue, New York, NY 10110

For information about special discounts for bulk purchases, please contact
W. W. Norton Special Sales at specialsales@wwnorton.com or 800-233-4830

Book design by Faceout Studio, Paul Nielsen

The Countryman Press
www.countrymanpress.com

A division of W. W. Norton & Company, Inc.
500 Fifth Avenue, New York, NY 10110
www.wwnorton.com

Library of Congress Cataloging-in-Publication Data

Aron, Jules, author.
  Zen and tonic : savory and fresh cocktails for
the enlightened drinker / Jules Aron.
    pages cm
  Includes index.
  ISBN 978-1-58157-307-7
1. Cocktails. I. Title.

TX951.A6765 2016
641.87'4—dc23

                    2015031175

10 9 8 7 6 5 4 3 2

To all the green innovators, craft visionaries,
and artisan trailblazers raising the bar on
organic, locally sourced, quality products.

Here's to infusing healthy, nutritious
ingredients back into our lives one
delicious drink at a time.

CONTENTS

INTRODUCTION

I love good, wholesome food.
Especially when paired with a fresh, crisp cocktail.

Nothing warms my heart like a table full of my favorite people sharing a flavorful meal and a few delicious drinks.

I love it so much, that I do it for a living.

I am a lifestyle and nutrition coach and The Healthy Bartender.

By combining my years of food and beverage industry experience with my passion for healthy ingredients, I create fun, simple, and delicious ways for you to live your best life ever. Like infusing nutritious ingredients back into your life one delicious drink at a time. And that's what this book is all about. So you can go ahead, grab some friends and loved ones, share a great meal, and actually drink to your health!

Spirited history

Drinking to good health might sound like an oxymoron, but a closer look at the history of spirits shows that alcohol has been used for over 1,000 years as the most efficient medium for delivering the medicinal properties of plants into our bloodstream. Healing ailments has always been at the root of cocktail culture. In fact, restorative cocktails were originally created in early pharmacies and apothecaries as early as the 16th century.

The earliest-known pharmacist-prepared tinctures, bitters, elixirs, and tonics were made with herbs, flowers, fruits, and yes, even vegetables laced with alcohol, which preserved their healing properties. These potions were custom made, using botanicals grown right in the apothecaries to ensure freshness and potency, then shaken or stirred and given to the patient as a prescription.

These restorative cocktails served people well, curing ailments ranging from an upset stomach to scurvy. In fact, what is simply known to modern cocktail lovers as a gin-and-tonic was first introduced by the British East India Company to prevent malaria among its soldiers in India.

It wasn't until 1906 that the government got involved and began to move alcohol-based cocktails out of pharmacies and into the cocktail bar, where their curative qualities became an afterthought.

Zen and tonic

I grew up drinking some very distinctive tonics every morning, thanks to my dad. He brewed herbal concoctions regularly to help strengthen my immunity. Although I didn't care much for them at the time, I did develop a strong appreciation for the health benefits of nutrient-rich herbs, spices, fruits, flowers, and vegetables. Since then, I've been playing hard to combine nutritious foods and boozy concoctions to create delectable recipes for health that keep food and life fun. So, get ready to experience the healing art of the cocktail that I like to call Zen and Tonic.

Stocking your home bar should be a fun and exciting venture. After all, you'll be using it to make many delicious libations from this book and beyond. For that reason, I've kept my suggestions and recommendations easy, affordable, and readily available.

In "The Fundamentals" (pages 14–15) is a list of essential bar and kitchen equipment, as well as glassware, to get you started. In "Spirits of Choice," pages 15–18, I provide a list of favorite organic spirits and mixers, and in " Drinks with Benefits," pages 21–27, I offer an introduction to the highly nutrient-dense foods we call superfoods. There are also discussions of ice and garnishes, and because there is no bigger buzz kill than artificial ingredients, all the products I choose have no artificial colors or flavors, high-fructose corn syrup, or refined sugar. Be sure to check out my sections on natural sweeteners, flavored syrups, and infused liquor recipes, which we'll use in the beverages. And then it's on to the cocktail recipes!

You'll also find a Resources section at the back of the book with a more comprehensive list of websites to help you source all the extras you might not find locally.

Say YES to:

Organic
Local
Seasonal
Fresh
Pure
Fun
Simple
Delicious
Made with love

Say NO THANKS to:

GMOs
Processed or packaged
Microwaveable
Bland or boring
Unpronounceable ingredients
Artificial colors or flavors
High-fructose corn syrup or refined sugar

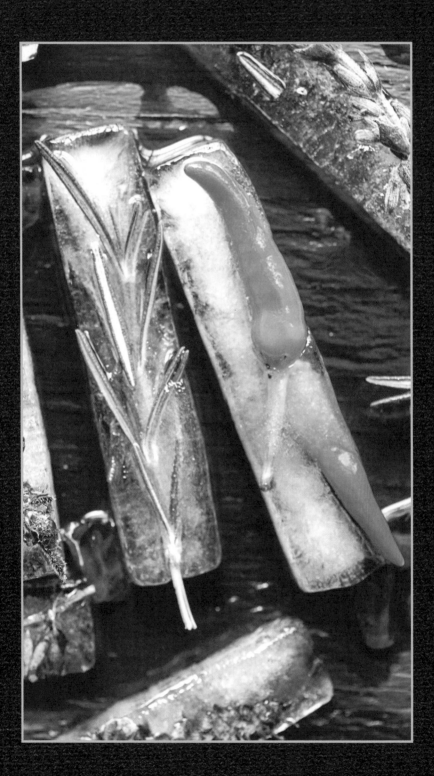

THE FUNDAMENTALS

Taking stock: Your essential bar tools,
kitchen equipment, and glassware

The equipment needed to mix a cocktail can be simple to master, and you don't need a lot of it. Here are the essentials:

BAR TOOLS AND KITCHEN EQUIPMENT

Bar spoon
Muddler
Jigger
Cocktail shaker
Strainer
Ice cube trays

Because we'll be using more fruits and vegetables, it's also essential to have a juicer, a blender, and a muddler, so that you can squeeze, blend, and mash all your delicious ingredients.

ESSENTIAL GLASSWARE

To keep things simple, I've narrowed down your glassware to five essentials:

The Collins (8–12 ounces)
The rocks glass (6–8 ounces)
The champagne flute
The martini glass (4–5 ounces)
The wine stem

You only need four to eight of each of these types.

Confused about all the different shapes of glasses?

Stemware is designed to keep fingers from warming up the glass.
The wider the mouth, the more the drink comes in
contact with oxygen, affecting the taste. The narrow opening of
champagne flutes keeps champagne sparkling, while the
wider bowl of martini glasses keeps the ingredients from separating.

Spirits of choice:
Why buy organic alcohol?

The alcohol you drink should be organic for the same reasons you'd buy organic food: to avoid artificial additives, and to help promote sustainable farming practices and environmentally friendly packaging—and because it tastes amazing, and its absence of chemicals lessens hangovers. If you're going to eat healthy, nutritious foods, your alcohol and mixers should be a pure, high-quality product as well.

Because no drink can ever rise above the quality of its ingredients, below are my 25 top picks for spirits, including wine, saké, and mixers for your home bar, with special attention given to small-batch, organic, and artisan producers that maintain sustainable practices and are impeccable with their ingredients.

Note: Many more great-quality products are listed in the Resources section at the back of the book.

Top 25 organic liquors and mixers to get you shaking

1. **Square One Vodka**—Square One helped pioneer organic hard-alcohol production when it released vodka made with certified organic American-grown rye in 2006. The company now has a few flavored varieties with a great one with infused organic cucumbers.

2. **Rain Organics Vodka**—Made from 100 percent organic white corn sourced from a single farm in Illinois and distilled in Kentucky, earning a Gold Medal at the San Francisco World Spirits Competition in 2010.

3. **Prairie Organic Vodka**—Another stellar organic vodka, Prairie is made in Minnesota, and stands out because the farmers who grow the corn for it also own the distillery, converting the leftover corncobs and other biomass into biogas to power the stills.

4. **4Copas Blanco Tequila**—This is a 100 percent agave tequila. The company also makes añejo, reposado, and special-release tequilas—including an añejo packaged in a pretty bottle decorated with a sea turtle, with all proceeds donated to sea turtle conservation.

5. **Del Maguey Single Village Mezcals**—Del Maguey makes "single village" mezcals; each is named for the town in which it's produced. The company claims to have always made its spirits organically, but it began the certification process in 2007.

6. **Casa Noble Tequila**—Award-winning Casa Noble is made from 100 percent organically farmed blue agave plants and is USDA-certified organic. All the tequila is made harvest-to-bottle on the Casa Noble estate, where water usage is carefully monitored and organic cleaning products dominate. Choose from silver, resposado, añejo, single-barrel resposado, and single-barrel añejo.

7. **Papagayo Organic Rums**—Papagayo's rums, available in white or spiced, are made in Paraguay from sugarcane grown on small family farms. Both rums are crafted with the highest standards for environmental sustainability, and social responsibility in mind, and are remarkably deep and crisp in flavor, earning them a 4-star rating from the *Spirits Journal*.

8. **Owney's NYC Rum**—White rum made from high-quality, all-natural, non-GMO molasses. Distilled in East Williamsburg, Brooklyn, New York.

9. **Bluecoat American Dry Gin**—A handcrafted, small-batch gin distilled in a copper pot, using only organic botanicals.

10. **Juniper Green Organic London Dry Gin**—This gin is made in London with juniper berries, coriander, angelica root, and savory. A bronze star winner at the International Wine & Spirit Competition.

11. **Benromach Organic Speyside Single Malt Scotch Whisky**—For fans of amber liquors, the organic options are slim. This single malt made in Speyside's smallest working distillery is one of the few. It is made from organic barley and yeast and is casked in virgin oak for at least three years.

12. **Balcones Whisky**—This Texas single-malt whisky defeated nine brands, including such famous Scottish houses as the Balvenie and the Macallan, in a blind panel of British spirits experts.

13. **Highland Harvest Organic Blended Scotch Whisky**—Made from a blend of three organic malts and an organic grain, this blended scotch has the nose of mature malt with gentle hints of age.

14. **Frey Organic Petite Sirah**—Winner of a gold medal at the 2010 Mendocino County Wine Competition, this organic petite sirah from America's first organic winery is free of added sulfites.

15. **Parducci Wine**—Parducci wines are not only affordable, they are made using organic grapes from family-owned farms and come delivered in eco-friendly packaging. The Parducci estate uses solar and renewable energy to power itself, as well as sustainable farming practices.

16. **Domaine Carneros Sparkling Wine**—Made from organic grapes, bubbly Domaine Carneros is also vegan. (If you didn't already know, champagne and sparkling wines have animal products, such as egg whites, in them.) The winery uses solar power and is a big fan of composting.

17. **Tarantas Organic Cava Brut**—This organic bubbly, produced by Spain's oldest estate winery, received a rating of 90 from *Wine & Spirits* magazine. Tarantas uses traditional cava grape varieties (Spain's answer to Champagne) to produce a pale yellow, creamy wine that the magazine lauded as "remarkably sophisticated for its price."

18. **Momokawa Organic Junmai Ginjo Nigori Saké**—From Oregon, USA. The first nigori saké to be certified organic.

19. **Akira Organic Junmai Saké**—From Ishikawa, Japan. Pure rice saké made from US NOP-certified organic rice. This saké is best described as a pioneering effort of a Japanese brewery trying to get USDA standards in Japan.

20. **Bison Brewing Organic India Pale Ale**—In 2010, Bison was selected as one of the top sustainable US breweries by *USA Today*. The company offsets its carbon footprint and makes four- and six-pack carriers from 100 percent recycled paper.

21. **Fever-Tree Sodas and Mixers**—This award-winning range of mixers now includes nine different flavors, including tonic, club soda, an outstanding ginger beer, and the elderflower tonic I use in my signature cocktail, Zen and Tonic (page 173).

22. **Ayala's Herbal Water**—Ayala's infuses organic herbal extracts in artesian water for an unusual mixer. The product is available in both still and sparkling formulations in a variety of flavors, such as lavender mint, ginger lemon peel, and lemongrass mint vanilla.

23. **Q Tonic**—Quality soda and tonic waters for cocktails.

24. **Bittermens Bitters and Spirits**—A New Orleans–based bitters company famous for a range of tinctures (grapefruit bitters, habanero shrub) and more experimental selections. They were once involved with Amor y Amargo, a tiny cocktail bar and bitters tasting room in New York City's East Village, where many of their products can still be found.

25. **The Spice Lab**—A great source for exotic salts. It has a mixology collection, and some fun Himalayan sea salt shot glasses.

Natural mixers

My philosophy as it pertains to drinks is the same as it applies to food: Fresh ingredients rule. *Organic, local, seasonal* are more than just buzzwords. They make excellent drinks. I use fresh herbs, spices, roots, fruits, and veggies from my neighbor's backyard, my own windowsill, or the weekly farmers' market. You can do the same. (Although I do recommend asking your neighbor first before you go rummaging through his garden patch! He'll certainly be on board after a sip of your delectable new drinks!)

When making cocktails with freshly squeezed, muddled, or blended herbs, fruits, and vegetables, it's especially important to go as natural as possible with all of your ingredients.

✦ ✦ ✦ ✦

Z&T TIP

Healthy foods are not always more expensive. Most comparison studies look at cost per calorie, not exactly the ideal when it comes to health. Especially when healthy fruits and veggies are usually lower in calories to begin with. To save money on these healthy options, buy in season and locally to save on shipping and middleman costs. And when organic is out of your price range, skip the fresh choices and opt for the frozen variety instead.

✦ ✦ ✦ ✦

Be a Label Junkie!

Next time you peel that sticker off your fruit, take a closer look. A four-digit PLU (price lookup) code means it's a conventional piece of fruit, likely grown with pesticides and depleted soil. A five-digit code beginning with an 8 indicates the fruit is a GMO and contains genetically modified organisms not naturally occurring in nature. The five-digit code beginning with a 9 is your best option, confirming that the fruit has been grown organically.

The following guidelines from the Environmental Working Group list the fruits and veggies grown with the highest pesticides levels and those with the lowest, so you can make better choices shopping for your ingredients.

FOODS TO BUY ORGANIC

Dirty Dozen Plus (produce with the highest pesticide loads): Apples, peaches, nectarines, strawberries, grapes, celery, spinach, sweet bell peppers, cucumbers, cherry tomatoes, imported snap peas, and potatoes. Plus leafy greens and hot peppers.

FOODS TO WORRY LESS ABOUT

Clean Fifteen (produce least likely to hold pesticide residues): Avocados, sweet corn, pineapples, cabbage, frozen sweet peas, onions, asparagus, mangoes, papayas, kiwis, eggplant, grapefruit, cantaloupe, cauliflower, and sweet potatoes.

DIY Produce Wash

1 cup water
1 cup white vinegar
1 tablespoon baking soda
½ cup lemon juice

Place all the ingredients in a bowl and stir to combine.
Pour into a spray bottle and spray produce before using.
Let sit for 5 minutes, rub with clean towel, rinse,
and enjoy.

DRINKS WITH BENEFITS

A look at the superstar superfoods that raise the bar on cocktails

A superfood is a nutrient-rich food considered to be especially beneficial for health and well-being. Although advertisers have been throwing around the word quite loosely these days, the concept behind the term remains quite real. A superfood is a food occurring naturally in nature that contains a high ratio of micronutrients to calories. These culinary superheroes are my cocktail superstars and they deserve a spotlight! Make sure to look for my **Superfood Spotlights** peppered throughout the book. Here are some highlights:

Açai berries

The açai berry was long cherished by the Amazonian people. This unique berry has an extraordinary amount of antioxidants that protect the tissues and cells of the body. The little açai berry also packs more grams of protein than an egg, and when combined with its host of omega-3 and -9 fatty acids, açai has been shown to improve the look and texture of your hair, skin, and nails.

Avocados

High in fat (the good kind), avocados may help reduce "bad" cholesterol levels. Also high in fiber and potassium.

Beets

This humble root vegetable holds a wealth of nutrients, including beta-carotene and folic acid, fiber, and iron. The leafy greens are even more nutritious, with double the potassium, folic acid, calcium, and iron.

Berries

Almost all berries rank among the world's most nutritious fruits. Their concentrated micronutrients make them one of the best sources of antioxidants.

Cacao

A prized food of the Mayans, cacao is the raw, natural source of one of the most cherished treats of all time: chocolate! And in its unprocessed form, cacao ranks as one of the most antioxidant-rich foods in the world. Cacao is also rich in minerals and is the top plant-based source of magnesium.

Carrots

Crunch your way to better vision, healthier kidneys, and a stronger liver with this sweet, bright root. Carrots also provide more of the health-promoting antioxidant, carotenoid, than does any other vegetable.

Chia seeds

A staple food for the Aztecs and Mayans, chia, which in ancient Mayan meant "strength," was a prized food that helped provide sustainable energy. The tiny seed is loaded with fiber, protein, omega-3 fatty acids, and a variety of micronutrients.

Citrus

Lemons, limes, oranges, and so on keep the body alkaline, help defend against the common cold, and fight inflammation.

Coconut water

This hydrating beverage, extracted from coconuts, is extremely rich in natural electrolytes, including calcium, magnesium, phosphorous, potassium, and sodium. It is also isotonic to human plasma, and has been used in extreme emergencies to quickly rehydrate the human body when administered intravenously.

When peeling citrus fruits, leave on the white pith, full of fiber-rich pectin, which helps lower your cholesterol.
And don't toss the peel if it's organic; the outermost layer, the zest, offers limonoids, a bitter-tasting lipid that protects the fruit from fungi and is a powerful carcinogen.

Dates

Dates contain selenium, manganese, copper, and magnesium, all of which are integral to healthy bone development and strength. They are also a great source of fiber, iron, vitamin A, and many B vitamins as well. They provide an instant energy boost and are one of the best sources of potassium.

Flowers (edible)

Long featured in natural remedies and homeopathic health treatments, flowers such as chamomile, marigold, elderflower, jasmine, lavender, hibiscus, and rose have been infused and distilled for centuries. They continue to be used in liqueurs and syrups, and I have included recipes for both.

Fruits and vegetables

Fruits and especially vegetables deserve more respect! For the small amount of calories they contain, they deliver the most nutrients of any class of food. How sad that in most households, vegetables are relegated to the corner of the plate, forced to be eaten because they "are good for us." Vegetables are an excellent low-calorie source of vitamins, minerals, and fiber, and it is time we see them in a new, delicious way!

The only rules when it comes to fruits and veggies are: Eat a wide variety, eat as organically as possible, and eat as many as possible.

Goji berries

Also called wolfberries, or "red diamonds" due to their unusually high nutritional value, Goji berries are fruits native to southeastern Europe and Asia. They are characterized by their bright orange-red color and raisinlike shape. They have been cultivated in Asia for over 2,000 years, where Traditional Chinese Medicine has used the berries for medicinal purposes. They are an excellent source of antioxidants, such as polyphenols, flavonoids, and carotenoids, as well as vitamins A, C, and E.

Green leafy vegetables

Exceptionally high in chlorophyll, these greens also contain large amounts of vitamins, minerals, protein, and fiber.

Try a different green at the market each week and explore the subtle differences between varieties, some mild, some bitter, and some spicy.

Herbs and spices

Just like leafy greens, herbs such as parsley and oregano can claim superfood status and contain medicinal properties.

Kiwis

Rich in vitamins C and E and lutein, kiwis may lower high cholesterol.

Kombucha

A fermented tea drink that has been a premium health tonic for centuries. Kombucha contains an exceptional quantity of energizing enzymes, vitamins, and beneficial bacteria. You can follow my recipe to make your own or pick up a batch at your local health food store or even your local kombucha bar, if you have one popping up in your 'hood.

How to Make Kombucha Tea at Home

Makes 1 gallon
1 gallon water, divided
8 green or black tea bags (I use organic)
1 cup organic sugar
1 SCOBY (kombucha starter)

Boil ½ gallon (8 cups) of the water in a large pot.
Add the tea bags and allow to steep for 20 minutes.
Remove the tea bags.
Add the sugar and stir well.
Allow the tea to come to room temperature and pour into
a clean 1-gallon mason jar or crock.
Add the remaining ½ gallon of water to the jar and
place the SCOBY in the jar.
Cover with cheesecloth, and secure with a rubber band.
Allow the homemade kombucha to ferment in a dark place
for 7 to 14 days.

Maqui berries

Maqui berries are the single highest-known antioxidant fruit in the world, with almost double the antioxidant activity of açai berries. They have a strong concentration of polyphenols and anthocyanins, which repair and protect DNA and improve brain function. Fresh maqui berries are not available in North America but a freeze-dried powder can be found online and in select stores.

Mushrooms

Of all the earth's natural substances, mushrooms are among the most medicinal. They enhance the immune system and fight free radicals.

Noni (juice)

Noni is high in phytonutrients, selenium, and vitamin C, which fights free radical damage on blood vessel walls. It also contains sco-poletin, a compound that may lower blood pressure. Moreover, the fruit is alkaline, which keeps bodily fluids from becoming too acidic, destroying free radicals.

Nuts and seeds

The embryo of all plants, nuts, and seeds are extremely high in life-sustaining nutrients, including healthy fats, minerals, protein,

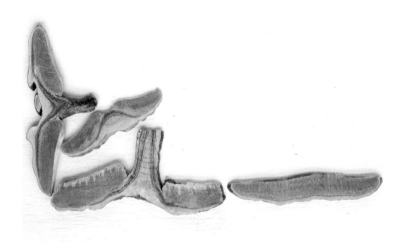

and fiber. Nuts and seeds can be blended into a healthy milk. I have included recipes for several milks in the "Rich and Creamy" section of the book (pages 205–229).

Papayas
Rich in antioxidants, papayas contain large amounts of vitamins A, C, and E, improving skin, nail, and hair. The fruit also contains large amounts of vitamin B_9, which aids in cell production and helps prevent anemia.

Pears
Pears lower LDL (bad) cholesterol that can reduce cardiovascular disease and diabetes. They also contain 6 grams of fiber, promoting healthy digestion and regulating blood sugar.

Pomegranates
With a long history of both medicinal and culinary uses, the pomegranate contains a broad spectrum of vitamins and minerals, such as vitamin C and potassium, and is packed with anti-inflammatory essential amino acids.

Sprouts
Sprouts are condensed nutrition at its finest and are easy to grow right on your kitchen countertop. Sprouts are incredibly rich in enzymes, vitamins, minerals, chlorophyll, antioxidants, and even protein.

Tomatoes
Tomatoes provide iron, potassium, fiber, a host of B vitamins, phytochemicals, and lycopene, associated with lowering the risk of macular degeneration; also, they lower the risk of coronary artery disease.

Wheatgrass
Wheatgrass is a sprout that grows from wheat. There are records of Ancient Egyptians' using wheatgrass for vitality purposes, which is not surprising. Composed of 70 percent chlorophyll, wheatgrass, and other supergrasses, such as barley grass and kamut grass, are exceptionally alkaline forming, supporting a healthy pH balance. And not to worry; despite their grain origin, the grasses are gluten free.

THE FUNDAMENTALS OF ICE

Ice serves two purposes in cocktail making: First, to chill the cocktail while shaking or stirring, while also diluting the drink ever so slightly to drinking perfection. Second, to keep the finished cocktail chilled while you enjoy it.

The type of ice you use when shaking and serving also dramatically affects your drink.

Ice cubes are used when you want to keep your drink cold without diluting it. Fresh 1- to 2-inch cubes work best: The larger the cube, the slower the melting process.

Crushed ice is used in stronger cocktails that are meant to be diluted. To make your own, simply fill a shaker one-third of the way with ice and muddle until broken up. Or use a bag to crush the ice.

Ice spheres: You can now purchase ice molds to make large ice spheres, which allow the flavor of your drink to open up without getting watered down too quickly. Filling the ice mold with edible blossoms can create a fragrant and attractive garnish.

Molds: Using fun-shaped molds can create interest in itself. I like to use leftover freshly squeezed juices and freeze them to add to my water, sodas, and spirits.

Punch wreaths: If you have a Bundt cake pan, you can fill it up with distilled water, citrus wheels, and an assortment of berries and

freeze it. Place it in the center of a punch bowl to cool and add flavor as the ice melts.

Flavored ice cubes are like jewelry for your drink—eye-catching and loaded with personality. They're also functional: As the cubes melt, they add hints of flavor, turning even a plain glass of water into an aromatic sip.

EDIBLE FLOWER ICE CUBES

Distilled water, boiled and cooled
12 culinary-grade edible flowers

Fill two extra-large ice cube trays about one-third full with the distilled water and add a flower facing down to each ice compartment. Freeze. Once frozen, fill two-thirds full with distilled water. Freeze again. Fill to the top with distilled water and freeze again.

CHERRY AND NONI JUICE ICE CUBES

1 cup cherry juice
½ cup noni juice

Combine the cherry and noni juice and pour into a large ice cube tray. Freeze for 4 to 6 hours. You will need these for the Tahitian Sunrise (page 111). The dark crimson ice cubes create a layered "sunrise" effect in the glass when the citrus juice is poured over it.

ALMOND MILK AND VANILLA ICE CUBES

2 cups almond milk
⅓ cup coconut sugar
1 vanilla bean or one teaspoon organic extract

Combine the almond milk and coconut sugar in a large saucepan. Slice open the vanilla bean lengthwise and scrape the insides into the saucepan, then place empty vanilla bean in the mixture. Bring to a simmer over medium heat, whisking to break up any clumps of vanilla. Once the mixture has come to a simmer, reduce the heat to low and cook for 10 minutes more, whisking occasionally.

Allow the vanilla mixture to come to room temperature. Pour through a fine-mesh strainer into a bowl with a spout, then pour the mixture into ice cube trays. Freeze until completely solid, 3 to 4 hours. Serve with the Lady Grey (page 171) or A Dash and a Wink (page 222), and any of your tea and coffee drinks.

Other ideas

You can freeze coconut water for your smoothies, pickled juices for your Bloody Mary, lemon mint for your water, and make hot chocolate, coffee, and tea ice cubes. You can even freeze aloe water—very useful, especially after a day of sipping on your new concoctions, poolside.

Z&T TIPS

· Ice is only good as the water it came from. Consider using filtered water, spring water, or boiled water to remove cloudiness.

· If you want your cocktails to look extra special, boil distilled water and let it cool before repeating the process. Pour your cooled water into an ice cube tray and freeze in a closed container. Your ice cubes will be clear and beautiful and won't pick up any flavors from your freezer.

· Infuse liquids as much as you can. The cold makes the flavors harder to taste.

· Spirits alone are harder to freeze, so mix them with other ingredients.

· Always strain your mixture before freezing, to avoid sediments settling at the bottom of the cubes.

✦ ✦ ✦ ✦

THE 101 ON
GARNISHES

Besides adding a decorative touch to your drink, garnishes should also provide integral, complementary flavors and aromas. A strategically placed citrus peel on a side of a drink that a guest can rub and squeeze will release just a touch of aroma to stimulate the senses. Edible flowers, fruit, berries, and leaves can also be wedged between ice cubes and the glass to create overall sensory impact. I use rose petals in a similar fashion in the Blushing Rose Sangria (page 177).

Citrus twists: Cut the ends off your citrus fruit and make an incision lengthwise, halfway through the fruit. Using your thumb, separate the rind from the flesh of your citrus fruit until you have removed the entire peel. Roll up the whole peel and cut into pieces to make curly twists.

Fans: You can make attractive fans from pears, apples, and strawberries. Simply pick a fruit with a firm flesh. Slice your fruit very thinly, leaving a tail at the bottom. Spread out the slices in a fan shape. Make sure to soak your fruit in lemon juice to prevent browning. I use a similar method for the pear garnish in the Pear and Lemongrass Soother (page 100).

Salt or sugar rims: Sugars and salts can be flavored with crushed flowers, herbs, and spices. Get creative! I use bee pollen to rim the glass of The Rejuvenator shot (page 89) and coconut flakes for the Bliss cocktail (page 221). I also love to use an assortment of pink

Himalayan and black Hawaiian salts and brown and flavored sugars. You'll find that the smaller the crystals, the easier to coat the rim. For salt or savory rims, cut a slot into a wedge of lime and gently rub around the rim of a glass before coating. For a sweet rim, do the same with a syrup.

LAVENDER SUGAR RIM

2 tablespoons culinary-grade lavender buds
1 cup coconut sugar, divided

Place the lavender buds and ¼ cup of the coconut sugar in a blender and grind until powdery. Mix with the remaining ¾ cup of coconut sugar and store in an airtight container.

ROSEBUD SUGAR RIM

2 tablespoons culinary-grade rosebuds
1 cup coconut sugar, divided

Place the rosebuds and ¼ cup of the coconut sugar in a blender and grind until powdery. Mix with the remaining ¾ cup of coconut sugar and store in an airtight container.

CINNAMON SUGAR RIM

3 tablespoons ground cinnamon
1 tablespoon orange zest
½ cup coconut sugar, divided

Place the cinnamon, orange zest, and ¼ cup of the coconut sugar in a blender and grind until slightly powdery. Mix with the remaining ¼ cup of coconut sugar and store in an airtight container.

LEMON SUGAR RIM

3 tablespoons pith-free lemon zest, dried overnight
1 cup coconut sugar, divided

Place the lemon zest and ¼ cup of the coconut sugar in a blender and grind until powdery. Mix with the remaining ¾ cup of coconut sugar and store in an airtight container.

CHILI SALT RIM

3 tablespoons red chili flakes or chili powder
1 tablespoon lime zest
½ cup Himalayan or sea salt, divided

Place the chili flakes, lime zest, and ¼ cup of the salt in blender and grind until slightly powdery. Mix with the remaining ¼ cup of salt and store in an airtight container.

CANDIED LAVENDER SPRIGS

12 culinary-grade lavender sprigs
½ cup Blueberry Lavender Syrup (page 38)
¼ cup Lavender Sugar Rim (page 35)
¼ cup Lemon Sugar Rim (page 35)

Gently coat each lavender sprig with the Blueberry Lavender Syrup and roll it in a mixture of Lavender Sugar Rim and Lemon Sugar Rim. Let dry on waxed paper for a few hours.

CANDIED ROSE PETALS

12 culinary-grade rose petals
½ cup Raspberry Rose Syrup (page 44)
¼ cup Rosebud Sugar Rim (page 35)
¼ cup Lemon Sugar Rim (page 35)

Gently dip each petal into the Raspberry Rose Syrup and then into a mixture of Rosebud Sugar Rim and Lemon Sugar Rim. Let dry on waxed paper for a few hours.

THE SWEET SPOT
OF SYRUPS

Sweetness is a key component to any good drink, helping balance acid, bitterness, and even alcohol. Swap your regular simple syrup and processed sugars for natural ones, for a healthy dose of sweet nutrients.

In addition to adding sweetness, cocktails made with syrups add a complexity and depth that you can taste: an extra hint of cinnamon, a floral undertone, a prick of heat, a fresh hint of mint. Here are a few worth trying out.

HIBISCUS SYRUP

1 cup water
1 cup pure maple syrup
¼ cup dried culinary-grade hibiscus flowers
1 (1-inch piece) ginger, peeled and grated

Combine the water, maple syrup, hibiscus, and ginger in a medium-size saucepan and bring to a boil, stirring frequently. Once at a boil, turn off the heat and allow the mixture to steep for at least 20 minutes, until all the maple syrup has dissolved and the syrup is deep magenta in color. Strain through a fine-mesh strainer. Transfer to a clean jar, cover, and keep refrigerated for up to 2 weeks.

DATE SYRUP

3 cups water
8 dates

Combine the water and dates in a medium-size saucepan. Simmer over medium-high heat for at least 10 minutes. Remove from the heat. Let cool to room temperature. Strain and enjoy. Store in the refrigerator for up to 2 weeks.

BLUEBERRY LAVENDER SYRUP

1 cup blueberries
1 cup honey
1 cup water
¼ cup culinary-grade lavender (organic, if available)

Combine all the ingredients in a small saucepan over medium-high heat. Bring to a boil, stir, and let boil until the honey has fully dissolved. Remove from the heat and let steep for 15 minutes. Pour through a fine-mesh strainer, pressing the blueberries to get all of their juices. Transfer to a clean jar, cover, and keep refrigerated for up to 2 weeks.

COCONUT SUGAR SIMPLE SYRUP

1 cup water
1 cup coconut sugar

Combine the water and coconut sugar in a medium-size saucepan. Stir. Heat over medium-high heat until it just starts to simmer. Remove from the heat. Let cool to room temperature. Transfer to a container and store in the refrigerator for up to 2 weeks.

✦ ✦ ✦ ✦

Coconut palm sugar, made from the nectar produced from the coconut tree, is a pure and simple low-glycemic sweetener. It is especially high in potassium, magnesium, zinc, and iron (as is coconut water) and is a natural source of the vitamins B_1, B_2, B_3, B_6, and C. It's also very rich in other minerals and enzymes that aid in its slow absorption into the bloodstream. When selecting your coconut sugar, please make sure that it is not mixed with cane sugar or malt-based ingredients.

✦ ✦ ✦ ✦

HONEY SYRUP

1 cup honey
1 cup water

Combine the honey and water in a small saucepan over medium heat and stir until the honey dissolves. Remove from the heat. Let cool to room temperature. Transfer to a clean glass jar, cover, and keep refrigerated for up to 2 weeks.

✦ ✦ ✦ ✦

According to Ayurvedic medicine, honey is revered as one of the five elixirs of immortality. Although, not a vegan option, honey has so many healing and restorative properties, it remains one of my top sweeteners of choice.

✦ ✦ ✦ ✦

JASMINE SYRUP

¼ cup culinary-grade dried jasmine buds
1 cup honey
1 cup water

Combine all the ingredients in a small saucepan over medium-high heat. Bring to a simmer and stir until the honey fully dissolves. Remove from the heat and let steep for 15 minutes. Strain into a clean jar, cover, and keep refrigerated for up to 2 weeks.

LILAC SYRUP

1 cup water
1 cup coconut sugar
2 cups culinary-grade lilac blossoms
Handful of blueberries or blackberries
1 tablespoon orange flower water
1 tablespoon freshly squeezed lemon juice

Combine the water and coconut sugar in a medium-size saucepan and stir over low heat until it boils. Add the lilac blossoms and berries and bring back to a boil. Add the orange flower water and lemon juice. Strain the liquid into a wide-mouth container while hot and funnel into a sealable bottle. Cover, and keep refrigerated for up to 2 weeks. Use in the Blueberry Lilac Granita (page 185).

APRICOT SYRUP

1 cup coconut sugar
1 cup water
3 pitted and quartered fresh apricots, or 6 ounces dried

Combine the coconut sugar and water in a small saucepan over medium-low heat. Add the apricots and let simmer slowly, stirring occasionally, for 20 minutes. Strain into a clean jar and refrigerate for 24 hours before using. Cover and keep refrigerated for up to 2 weeks.

BLACKSTRAP MOLASSES SIMPLE SYRUP

1 cup water
2 tablespoons blackstrap molasses

Combine the water and molasses in a medium-size saucepan. Stir. Heat over medium-high heat until it just starts to simmer. Do not bring to a boil. Overcooking the molasses will destroy its nutritional compounds. Remove from the heat. Let cool to room temperature. Transfer to a container and store in the refrigerator for up to 2 weeks. Use in the A Dash and a Wink cocktail (page 222).

✦ ✦ ✦ ✦

Blackstrap molasses contains less sugar than white sugar, brown sugar, regular molasses, or dark molasses, yet far more minerals and electrolytes. So, when you add a tablespoon of blackstrap molasses to your cocktail, you're getting more calcium than a cup of raw spinach, twice the potassium of a banana, and almost 100 mg of magnesium. Featuring a robust bittersweet flavor, blackstrap molasses is a fantastic sweetener that will add complexity and subtle sweetness to cocktails while also adding a dose of healthy nutrients to your libation.

✦ ✦ ✦ ✦

EUCALYPTUS SYRUP

1 cup water
1 cup pure maple syrup
¼ cup culinary-grade fresh eucalyptus leaves

Combine all the ingredients in a small saucepan over medium-high heat. Bring to a simmer and stir until the maple syrup fully dissolves. Remove from the heat and let steep for 15 minutes. Strain into a clean jar, cover, and keep refrigerated for up to 2 weeks.

RHUBARB SYRUP

1 cup honey
1 cup water
1 cup chopped fresh rhubarb (½-inch pieces; about 2 stalks)

Combine all the ingredients in a small saucepan and bring to a gentle boil, stirring occasionally. Lower the heat slightly and simmer for 20 minutes. Turn off the heat and allow the syrup to cool fully. Strain into a clean jar, cover, and keep refrigerated for up to 2 weeks.

ORANGE MARIGOLD SYRUP

¼ cup culinary-grade dried marigolds
1 cup honey
1 cup water
Zest and juice of ½ orange

Combine all the ingredients in a small saucepan over medium-high heat. Bring to a simmer and stir until the honey fully dissolves. Remove from the heat and let steep for 15 minutes. Strain into a clean jar, cover, and keep refrigerated for up to 2 weeks.

MAPLE SIMPLE SYRUP

1 cup water
1 cup pure maple syrup

Combine the water and maple syrup in a medium-size saucepan. Stir. Heat over medium-high heat until it just starts to simmer. Remove from the heat. Let cool to room temperature. Transfer to a container and store in the refrigerator for up to 2 weeks.

✦ ✦ ✦ ✦

*This natural sweetener features over 54 antioxidants that can help delay or prevent diseases caused by free radicals. Maple syrup is also high in zinc and manganese, keeping the heart healthy and boosting the immune system.
Make sure to buy 100 percent pure maple syrup, not pancake syrup.*

✦ ✦ ✦ ✦

LEMONGRASS SYRUP

1 cup water
1 cup honey
2 lemongrass stalks, sliced

Combine the water, honey, and lemongrass in a small saucepan. Simmer over medium heat for 10 minutes, until the honey is dissolved. Remove from the heat and let cool to room temperature. Strain into a clean jar, cover, and keep refrigerated for up to 2 weeks.

✦ ✦ ✦ ✦

Z&T TIP

To preserve your syrups for longer periods of time, add a splash of vodka.

✦ ✦ ✦ ✦

RASPBERRY ROSE SYRUP

1 cup raspberries
¼ cup culinary-grade dried rose petals
1 cup boiling water
¼ teaspoon rose water
1 cup honey

Steep the raspberries and rose petals in the boiling water for 15 minutes. Strain and lightly squeeze to extract any excess water. Add the rose water and honey and stir until dissolved. Strain into a clean jar, cover, and keep refrigerated for up to 2 weeks.

PEAR GINGER SYRUP

1 cup pure maple syrup
1 cup cored and chopped pear
2 tablespoons chopped fresh ginger
1 cup water
1 vanilla bean, or a splash of pure vanilla extract

Combine all the ingredients in a small saucepan over medium-high heat. Lower the heat and simmer for 20 minutes. Remove from the heat and let cool to room temperature. Strain into a clean jar, cover, and keep refrigerated for up to 2 weeks.

PASSION FRUIT SYRUP

1 cup honey
1 cup water
½ cup passion fruit pulp and juice

Combine the ingredients in a saucepan over low heat and bring to a boil. Let sit for 30 minutes to cool. Strain into a clean jar, cover, and keep refrigerated for up to 2 weeks.

ROSEMARY SAGE SYRUP

1 cup honey
1 cup water
Several sprigs each of rosemary and sage

Combine all the ingredients in a small saucepan and bring to a gentle boil, stirring occasionally. Lower the heat slightly and simmer for 5 minutes. Turn off the heat and allow the syrup to cool fully. Strain into a clean jar, cover, and keep refrigerated for up to 2 weeks.

INFUSED SPIRITS

Infusing spirits with flavor is a great way to experiment with your own personal tastes. The basic concept is to marry a variety of choice flavors into a base liquor to create a custom-flavored spirit. You can give your spirit a subtle hint of spice or deep, aromatic notes of flavor simply by choosing how long you let your infusion sit. Follow these guidelines for best results:

- Strong flavors, such as hot peppers, vanilla pods, and lavender buds, only need a few hours to a day.
- Fresh herbs, ginger, and citrus peels need 1 to 3 days, tops.
- Most fruits and berries need 3 to 6 days.
- Vegetables and hardy fruits, such as apples and pears, need 5 to 7 days.

Here are some recipes to get you started. We'll use them in some of the cocktail recipes.

CUCUMBER INFUSED GIN

1 large cucumber

1 cup gin

Peel, seed, and chop the cucumber. Place in a large glass container with a tight-fitting lid.

Pour the gin over the cucumber. Seal and let sit for 3 to 6 days. Shake periodically to distribute the flavors.

Strain and store. Try using the "pickled" cucumber as garnish in the Garden Variety (page 133).

GOJI BERRY INFUSED VODKA

1 cup vodka
½ cup dried goji berries

Combine the vodka and goji berries in a sealable glass jar and store in
a dark, cool place for 1 week. Shake periodically to distribute the flavors. Remove the goji berries. (I would recommend adding the gojis
to the Superfruit Sangria, page 76).

Strain and store.

ROSE INFUSED GIN

1 cup gin
2 tablespoons culinary-grade rosebuds

Add the rosebuds to the gin and let sit overnight, covered, at room temperature.

Strain and store.

ORANGE INFUSED VODKA

1 cup vodka
1 tablespoon orange zest, pith removed

Combine the vodka and orange zest in a sealable glass jar and store in a cool, dark place for 3 days.

Strain and store.

Note: The longer it infuses, the more bitter it will get.

THYME AND CHILE INFUSED TEQUILA

Handful of fresh thyme
6 small chiles
1 cup tequila

Combine the thyme, chiles, and tequila in a sealable glass jar and let infuse overnight. Shake periodically to distribute the flavors.

Strain and store.

CHERRY INFUSED BOURBON

1 cup fresh cherries
1 cup bourbon

Score each cherry with a knife, piercing through the flesh. No need to pit them. Combine the scored cherries and bourbon in a sealable glass jar, and allow to infuse for 2 to 4 weeks.

Strain and store.

Keep the bourbon-soaked cherries to garnish your drinks and even your desserts. You'll never have another maraschino cherry again!

VANILLA INFUSED RUM

2 vanilla pods

1 cup rum

Slit each vanilla pod gently down the middle.

Combine the vanilla pods with the rum in a sealable glass jar. Let sit for a week or longer.

Store it in a cool, dry place that is not affected by light.

Give the bottle a gentle shake now and then to help distribute the infusion.

Strain and store.

Variation: Add cacao nibs for delicious hints of dark chocolate!

A Final Note

All this healthy talk as it pertains to drinking wouldn't be complete without the word moderation.

Fresh ingredients, organic spirits, and homemade recipes do make delicious cocktails with healing properties, but a cocktail a day will not cure any disease. Nor will six or seven.

However, while enjoying a cocktail, why not make it a delicious one, blended with fresh ingredients and loads of health benefits?

Simply put, know your limits and know that drinking excessively, no matter what the drink, is not healthy.

With that said, let's make some drinks!

Unless noted otherwise, each recipe is for one serving.

LUSH AND FRUITY

The delightfully fresh fruits showcased

in the following libations will have

your taste buds rejoicing.

SUMMER THYME

This quintessential summer cocktail, bursting with fresh, juicy strawberries, gets a touch of sophistication with the penetrating herbal fragrance of fresh thyme. It pairs amazingly well with gin's botanical notes; however, if you are not a gin lover, you can easily replace the gin with vodka or experiment further by mixing the cocktail with a bolder tequila.

¼ cup strawberries
3 thyme sprigs
1 lemon wedge
3 ounces gin

Place the strawberries, two of the thyme sprigs and the lemon wedge in a shaker and muddle well; alternatively, you can juice them, fill the shaker with ice, add the gin, and shake well. Double strain into a chilled martini glass and garnish with the remaining thyme sprig.

✦ ✦ ✦ ✦

SUPERFOOD SPOTLIGHT

With antibacterial properties and high amounts of vitamins, thyme has a long history of use in natural medicine in connection with chest and respiratory problems.

✦ ✦ ✦ ✦

PAPAYA PASSION FRESCA

Common throughout Latin America, agua frescas, made by blending fresh fruit or veggies with cold water, are the ultimate hot-weather refreshers, but you don't need to cross the border to get a taste for yourself. This papaya fresca, made with coconut water, aloe water, lime juice, passion fruit syrup, and tequila, is just the ticket for a home-thrown fiesta of your own.

MAKES 6 TO 8 SERVINGS

5 cups ripe papaya (once peeled and chopped)
2 cups coconut water
2 cups aloe water
1 cup Passion Fruit Syrup (page 46)
½ cup freshly squeezed lime juice
2 cups tequila

Peel the papaya and slice in half lengthwise. Scoop out the seeds and fibrous part with a small spoon and discard.

Give the fruit a rough chop and transfer to a blender. Working in batches, combine the chopped papaya, coconut water, aloe water, syrup, and lime juice. Blend on high speed until the mixture is completely liquid.

Transfer the papaya mixture to a pitcher. Add the tequila and stir to combine.

Fill six to eight glasses with ice cubes. Pour the agua fresca into the glasses.

✦ ✦ ✦ ✦

SUPERFOOD SPOTLIGHT

Enjoy this agua fresca knowing it is a rich source of such antioxidant nutrients as carotenes, vitamin C, and flavonoids; vitamins B_5 and B_9; the minerals potassium, copper, and magnesium; and fiber.

✦ ✦ ✦ ✦

TROPICAL BREEZE

This tropical punch, chock-full of alkalizing and antioxidant-rich fruit, makes a favorite summer selection.

MAKES 6 TO 8 SERVINGS

1 pineapple, cut into cubes

1 lemon

2 limes

3 oranges

6 cups peeled and sliced kiwi

4 cups coconut water

2 cups rum

Reserve 2 wheels of each fruit to garnish the punch bowl. Using a juicer, process the remaining pineapple, lemon, lime, oranges, and kiwi. Whisk and pour into a large punchbowl and chill. Before serving, add the reserved fruit, coconut water, and rum.

✦ ✦ ✦ ✦

Z&T TIP

This is the perfect punch from which to create an ice wreath. Simply freeze the reserved fruit in a Bundt pan, following the instructions on page 29.

✦ ✦ ✦ ✦

CRIMSON SMASH

Rum's the word in this icy smash of raspberries and intoxicating hibiscus syrup.

¼ cup raspberries
8 fresh mint leaves
5 lime wedges
¾ ounce Hibiscus Syrup (page 37)
2 ounces white rum
Splash of soda water

Place the raspberries, mint, and two of the lime wedges in a sturdy glass. Muddle. Add two more of the lime wedges and the hibiscus syrup, and muddle again to release the juices. Do not strain the mixture. Fill the glass almost to the top with ice. Pour the rum over the ice, and fill the glass with soda water. Stir and garnish with the remaining lime wedge. Try Fever-Tree's lemon tonic for an added zing of flavor.

✦ ✦ ✦ ✦

SUPERFOOD SPOTLIGHT

This vibrant drink is as nutritionally powerful as it is colorful. The raspberry provides us with antioxidant and anti-inflammatory phytonutrients of greater diversity than those in most fruits.

✦ ✦ ✦ ✦

KIWI SOOTHER

Not too sweet, this remarkably thirst-quenching, crisp, green refresher is the perfect escape on a hot summer day.

2 ounces tequila
1 cup kiwi, peeled
½ cup aloe water
⅓ cup freshly squeezed lime juice
½ ounce Lemongrass Syrup (page 43)

Place all the ingredients in a blender and blend until smooth. Add ice and blend once more.

✦ ✦ ✦ ✦

SUPERFOOD SPOTLIGHT

This cleansing duo helps eliminate toxins from our body and keeps our electrolytes in balance.

✦ ✦ ✦ ✦

MARMALADE SKY

Drinks made with marmalade date to at least 1930, when the gin-based marmalade cocktail appeared in Harry Craddock's *The Savoy Cocktail Book* as a morning tipple. Delicious, citrusy, and refreshing, this drink provides a quick wake-up call any time of day. My version only tastes like marmalade. I use fresh and dried fruits to replicate the taste without the unnecessary sugars.

1 pitted nectarine or small peach
¾ ounce Apricot Syrup (page 40)
3 orange wedges, or ¼ cup freshly squeezed orange juice
2 ounces rum
¼ cup brewed green tea, chilled
Orange slice, for garnish

Place the nectarine, syrup, and orange wedges in a shaker and muddle. Fill the shaker with ice and add the rum. Shake and double strain into a glass with fresh ice. Top with the chilled green tea. Garnish with an orange slice.

✦ ✦ ✦ ✦

SUPERFOOD SPOTLIGHT

Peaches, the fuzzy natives of China, are packed with numerous health-promoting compounds, minerals, and vitamins, while the green tea increases the antioxidant levels in this refreshing iced tea.

✦ ✦ ✦ ✦

SPRING FLING

Welcome spring the right way with this bright, colorful punch.
MAKES 6 TO 8 SERVINGS

4 cups water
1½ cups raspberries
1½ cups chopped rhubarb
1½ cups strawberries
4 beets
1 lemon
½ cup Raspberry Rose Syrup (page 44)
2 cups whiskey
1 cup kombucha

In a saucepan, bring the water, raspberries, rhubarb, and strawberries to a boil. Lower the heat and simmer for 15 minutes. Strain through a sieve, pressing to extract all the liquid. Discard the solids. Chill.

Using a juicer, process the beets and lemon. Place in a punch bowl, and whisk in the chilled fruit mixture. Add the rose syrup and whiskey. Top off with the kombucha for some extra effervescence.

✦ ✦ ✦ ✦

SUPERFOOD SPOTLIGHT

Kombucha is an age-old fermented tea drink that has been around for centuries. It contains a variety of vitamins, minerals, and enzymes, and has been prized by traditional cultures for its health-promoting properties, including liver detoxification, digestion, and nutrient assimilation.

✦ ✦ ✦ ✦

CHERRY COCONUT CHILLER

Hydrating coconut water, thirst-quenching lime juice, and antioxidant-rich cherries make this the ultimate summer refresher.
MAKES 6 TO 8 SERVINGS

4 cups coconut water
4 cups cherries, pitted
6 tablespoons chia seeds
1 cup freshly squeezed lime juice
2 cups rum
Unsweetened shredded coconut, for garnish

Place all the ingredients, except the rum and shredded coconut, in a blender and purée until well combined. Pour into a pitcher and mix with the rum. Serve over ice and sprinkle with shredded coconut.

✦ ✦ ✦ ✦

SUPERFOOD SPOTLIGHT

Despite their tiny size, chia seeds are among the most nutritious foods on the planet. They are loaded with fiber, protein, Omega-3 fatty acids, and various micronutrients.
Cherries contain fiber, vitamin C, carotenoids, and anthocyanins. They are also anti-inflammatory and may help reduce pain and inflammation in the body.

✦ ✦ ✦ ✦

BERRY QUEEN

Dark berries reign supreme in this antioxidant-rich frozen elixir.

2 ounces gin
¼ cup blackberries, frozen
¼ cup blueberries, frozen
¼ cup pomegranate juice

Place all the ingredients in a blender and blend until smooth. Add ice and blend once more.

✦ ✦ ✦ ✦

SUPERFOOD SPOTLIGHT

Dark berries are known to promote the healthy tightening of skin tissue as well as help maintain clarity of thought and good memory.

✦ ✦ ✦ ✦

RED LYCHEE DAIQUIRI

The original daiquiri was a mixture of rum, lime, and sugar, served over ice. Constantino Ribalaigua, the famed bartender at Havana's La Floridita—nicknamed *La Catedral del Daiquiri*—blended the drink with shaved ice, thereby creating the frozen daiquiri.

Ripe raspberries, sweet lychees, tangy rhubarb, and light notes of rose water make this frozen daiquiri a delightful experience.

1½ ounces rum
½ cup fresh or frozen raspberries
6 to 8 fresh lychees, peeled and pitted
½ ounce fresh lime juice
1½ ounces Rhubarb Syrup (page 42)
Splash of rose water (optional)

Place all the ingredients in a high-speed blender and blend until smooth. Serve immediately.

SUPERFRUIT SANGRIA

Sangria, the sweet and savory Spanish punch made with wine and sweetened seasonal fruits, is always the hit of the party. Here's how to infuse this favorite party pleaser with an assortment of superberries, for a fun and healthy new flavor combination.

MAKES 8 TO 10 SERVINGS

2 (750 ml) bottles red wine
1 cup blackberries
1 cup raspberries
1 cup strawberries
¼ cup dried goji berries
1 cup pomegranate juice
½ cup freshly squeezed grapefruit juice
1 lemon, cut into wheels
1 lime, cut into wheels
1 orange, cut into wheels
Sparkling water, organic lemon soda, kombucha,
or sparkling wine, for serving

Combine all the ingredients, except the sparkling water, in a large pitcher and refrigerate overnight. Add the sparkling water before serving. Make sure to distribute the fruit evenly in the cups for extra delicious servings of superfruits.

✦ ✦ ✦ ✦

SUPERFOOD SPOTLIGHT

This sangria is rich in polyphenol resveratrol, the heart-healthy and antiaging antioxidant.

✦ ✦ ✦ ✦

Z&T TIP

A few simple twists are all you need to bring your sangria to fresh new heights. The type of wine you choose will determine the flavor you'll create, so here are a few guidelines:

Pinot noir, *with notes of cherry, pairs beautifully with bright herbs, such as basil, and lighter red fruits, such as cherries, raspberries, and cranberries.*

Cabernet, *bold and muscular, works well with peppercorns, blackberries, and cinnamon.*

Shiraz, *smoky and peppery, suits blueberries, vanilla, star anise, and cloves wonderfully.*

Sauvignon blanc, *light and grassy, doesn't overpower kiwis, limes, and honeydew.*

Riesling, *sweet and crisp, is a good match for ginger, peach, and mangoes.*

Prosecco, *crisp and sparkling, complements citrus, tangerine, blood orange, and strawberries.*

✦ ✦ ✦ ✦

ISLAND SUNSET

This showstopper, the color of a tropical sunset, will whisk you away to the islands.

2 ounces rum
½ mango, pitted, cubed, and frozen
½ papaya, seeded, cubed, and frozen
⅓ cup freshly squeezed Key lime juice
1 tablespoon goji berries, plus more for garnish

Place all the ingredients, except the goji berry garnish, in a blender and blend until smooth. Add ice and blend once more. Top with the reserved goji berries.

✦ ✦ ✦ ✦

SUPERFOOD SPOTLIGHT

Papayas offer not only the luscious taste and sunlit color of the tropics, but are rich sources of antioxidant nutrients such as carotene, vitamin C, and flavonoids; the B vitamins, folate, and pantothenic acid; the minerals, potassium, copper, and magnesium; and fiber. Together, these nutrients promote the health of the cardiovascular system. Similarly, mangoes are an excellent source of powerful antioxidants that are also rich in tartaric acid, malic acid, and traces of citric acid, that help keep the body alkaline.

✦ ✦ ✦ ✦

WATERMELON CHIA FRESCA

What is more refreshing than a big chilled wedge of watermelon on a hot, summer day? Watermelon chia fresca, of course! Traditionally made from soaked chia seeds combined with water or citrus juice, this fresca is paired with refreshing watermelon, hibiscus, and basil for an intoxicatingly refreshing sipper.

MAKES 6 TO 8 SERVINGS

6 tablespoons chia seeds
2 cups water
6 cups cubed, seeded watermelon
15 fresh basil leaves
1 cup freshly squeezed lime juice
1 cup Hibiscus Syrup (page 37)
2 cups vodka

Combine the chia seeds and water in a glass and stir well. Allow the mixture to sit for 10 minutes. Stir once more and set aside for another 10 minutes.

Place all the ingredients, except the vodka, in a blender and blend until well combined. Pour into a pitcher and mix with the vodka. Serve over ice.

✦ ✦ ✦ ✦

SUPERFOOD SPOTLIGHT

The unassuming chia adds fiber, omega fatty acids, calcium, antioxidants, and even protein to this lovely elixir. It's no wonder the Aztecs and Maya considered chia seeds to be magical, for their ability to increase stamina and energy over long periods of time.

The watermelon packs quite an impressive nutritional punch as well. This melon is high in vitamin C, calcium, magnesium, fiber, protein, and a very large amount of potassium. Furthermore, it contains vitamin A; vitamins B_1, B_3, and B_6; and a wide variety of carotenoids and phytonutrients, including lycopene.

✦ ✦ ✦ ✦

BEET BERRY BOMB

These stunning fuchsia shots, with their velvety smooth texture, are the showstoppers you need at your next gathering.

MAKES 4 SHOTS

4 beets
2 apples
1 cup frozen raspberries
4 ounces gin

In a juicer, process the beets and apples and transfer to a blender. Add the frozen raspberries and blend.

Transfer the mixture to a shaker filled with ice, add the gin, and shake well.

✦ ✦ ✦ ✦

SUPERFOOD SPOTLIGHT

This bright vibrant shot provides antioxidant, anti-inflammatory, and detoxification support.

✦ ✦ ✦ ✦

STRAWBERRY GUAVA MARGARITA

You'll be hard-pressed to resist the sweet and tart flavors of this tropical cooler.

2 ounces tequila
½ cup strawberries, frozen
½ cup guava, pitted
½ ounce freshly squeezed lime juice

Place all the ingredients in a blender and blend until smooth.

✦ ✦ ✦ ✦

SUPERFOOD SPOTLIGHT

Apart from their distinctive flavor and lovely aroma, guavas are one of the richest sources of vitamin C, a vitamin that helps protect us against common infections and pathogens. The guava works in harmony with the ruby red strawberry, making this a powerful immunity-boosting elixir.

✦ ✦ ✦ ✦

BEACH PLUM

The sweet blackberry and the tart plum make for a vibrant flavor combination worthy of any occasion.

2 ounces gin
½ cup diced and pitted plum
½ cup blackberries, frozen
½ ounce freshly squeezed lime juice

Place all the ingredients in a blender and blend until smooth. Add ice and blend once more.

✦ ✦ ✦ ✦

Z&T VARIATION

Plums pair nicely with gin (think sloe gin). However, this deep berry delight is equally delicious with rum, vodka, and yes, whiskey! Have fun!

✦ ✦ ✦ ✦

THE
REJUVENATOR

This delicious shot will rejuvenate your senses and boost your energy.

MAKES 4 SHOTS

1 tablespoon bee pollen granules
3 ounces pomegranate juice
4 ounces whiskey

Rim four shot glasses with bee pollen. In a shaker filled with ice, combine the pomegranate juice and whiskey. Shake well and pour into the prepared shot glasses.

✦ ✦ ✦ ✦

SUPERFOOD SPOTLIGHT

Bee pollen is an energy booster and a powerful immune system builder and supports the cardiovascular system.

✦ ✦ ✦ ✦

TROPICAL BEET

Tap into the tropical sweetness of this golden-hued shot. It can't be beet!

MAKES 4 SHOTS

1 cup cubed mango
1 cup quartered golden beet
½ ounce freshly squeezed lime juice
4 ounces tequila

In a juicer, process the mango and beet. Transfer the mixture to an ice-filled shaker, add the lime juice and tequila, and shake vigorously. Divide among four shot glasses.

✦ ✦ ✦ ✦

SUPERFOOD SPOTLIGHT

Golden beets tend to be a bit sweeter and taste a little less earthy than red beets. Paired with the sweet mango, this humble root vegetable goes completely unnoticed, yet its powerful contribution does not. The golden beet is heart-healthy, and is an excellent kidney and internal body cleanser.

✦ ✦ ✦ ✦

SUPERBERRY BOOSTER

This berry delightful shot will boost you to new heights.

MAKES 4 SHOTS

2 cups cherries, pitted
½ ounce freshly squeezed lime juice
4 ounces Goji Berry Infused Vodka (page 51)
1 tablespoon açai powder

In a juicer, process the cherries and limes and transfer to a blender.
Add the vodka and açai powder and blend until well combined.

✦ ✦ ✦ ✦

SUPERFOOD SPOTLIGHT

*This antioxidant shot helps minimize damage to cells and helps
your body protect itself from oxidation. Açai can provide up to 30 times
the amount of anthocyanins in red wine and all the beneficial fatty acids
of olive oil in one all-natural and delicious shot.*
*Açai contains large amounts of plant sterols, which have been shown
to reduce cholesterol.*

✦ ✦ ✦ ✦

STRAWBERRY FIELDS

Let this sweet berry shot dazzle your taste buds.

MAKES 4 SHOTS

1 cup strawberries
1 large handful spinach
1 tablespoon chia seeds
4 ounces rum

In a juicer, process the strawberries and spinach. Transfer the mixture to a container. Add the chia seeds, stir, and let sit for 10 minutes to allow the chia seeds to swell. Shake again and let sit for an additional 10 minutes. Transfer the mixture to an ice-filled shaker, add the rum, and divide among four shot glasses.

✦ ✦ ✦ ✦

SUPERFOOD SPOTLIGHT

You can barely detect the spinach in this shot. Yet the benefits are remarkable. Spinach is a good source of vitamins A, B$_2$, B$_9$, C, and K, and contains magnesium, manganese, iron, calcium, and potassium.

✦ ✦ ✦ ✦

FRESH AND CRISP

These delightfully bright libations

will intoxicate you with their

vibrant freshness.

THE SPARKLING SAGE

This sophisticated sparkler boasts the sweetness and amazing anti-oxidant properties of the blackberry, while savory sage, considered to be an outstanding memory enhancer, lends subtle yet enchanting herbal notes.

⅓ ounce freshly squeezed lemon juice
¼ ounce Honey Syrup (page 39)
1 cup blackberries
2 or 3 fresh sage leaves, plus 1 for garnish
4 ounces sparkling wine

Combine the lemon, honey, blackberries, and two or three sage leaves in a glass and muddle well. Transfer the puréed mixture to a champagne flute and top off with the sparkling wine.

Garnish the flute with the reserved sage leaf.

PEAR AND LEMONGRASS SOOTHER

Despite its simplicity, this delicate and well-balanced drink feels sophisticated and particularly soothing.

2 pears, plus 1 stemmed and cored pear, for garnish (optional)
2 green apples
½ ounce freshly squeezed lemon juice
3 ounces saké
1 lemongrass stalk, plus more for garnish (optional)
½ ounce Lemongrass Syrup (page 43)

Using a juicer, process the two pears, apples, and lemon juice. Transfer to an ice-filled shaker, add the saké and lemongrass syrup, and shake vigorously. Double strain the mix into a glass and garnish with lemongrass and/or a fanned pear.

✦　✦　✦　✦

Z&T VARIATION

This is a wonderfully soothing cocktail to try warm! Simply transfer the pear mixture to a saucepan and heat over medium heat, stirring in the syrup. Bring to just under a boil. Cover, lower the heat, simmer for a few minutes, then add the saké. Enjoy on a cold fall evening!

✦　✦　✦　✦

SUPERFOOD SPOTLIGHT

The phytonutrient-rich pear provides us with antioxidant as well as anti-inflammatory benefits, while the aromatic lemongrass is chock-full of antibacterial, antifungal, and antimicrobial properties that will help keep you healthy all through the cold season.

✦ ✦ ✦ ✦

RUBY ROSE

Tart and tangy with an underlying sweetness, the grapefruit sparkles with health-promoting benefits.

6 Ruby Red grapefruit segments, plus 1 segment for garnish
½ ounce Rosemary Sage Syrup (page 47)
2 ounces whiskey
Rosemary sprig, for garnish

Muddle the six grapefruit segments and add the syrup. Transfer to an ice-filled shaker and add the whiskey. Shake and pour the contents into a glass.

Garnish with a rosemary sprig and the reserved grapefruit segment.

✦ ✦ ✦ ✦

SUPERFOOD SPOTLIGHT

An excellent source of vitamin C, grapefruit protects from free radicals and reduces inflammation. Rosemary, the fragrant evergreen, meanwhile stimulates the immune system, increases circulation, and improves digestion.

✦ ✦ ✦ ✦

CIDER HOUSE RULES

This crisp apple cider margarita will tantalize your senses.

Several fennel fronds, plus 1 more for garnish
1 cup organic apple cider
½ ounce Honey Syrup (page 39)
⅓ ounce freshly squeezed lime juice
1½ ounces silver tequila
Cinnamon Sugar (page 35)

In a shaker, muddle a few fennel fronds. Add the apple cider, syrup, lime juice, tequila, and ice and shake vigorously. Rim your glass with Cinnamon Sugar, fill a glass with ice, and strain the blend into the glass. Garnish with the reserved fennel frond.

✦ ✦ ✦ ✦

Z&T VARIATION

This is another excellent drink to try warm on a cold, winter day. In a medium-size saucepan, bring the apple cider, fennel, and syrup to just under a boil. Simmer for 5 minutes. Add the lime juice and tequila and mix. Strain the blend and pour into two glasses rimmed with Cinnamon Sugar. Garnish with additional fennel.

SUPERFOOD SPOTLIGHT

Cider is an unpasteurized, unfiltered juice made from apple mash, containing the juice with sediment and pulp from the fruit. Apples are a healthy, nutritious food and cider offers a distinctive way to take advantage of some of their benefits.

✦ ✦ ✦ ✦

GREEN ORCHARD

Hail to the kale with this sophisticated green martini paired with crisp apples and pears.

1 pear
1 green apple
4 to 6 kale leaves
¼ ounce freshly squeezed lemon juice
2 ounces vodka
½ ounce Pear Ginger Syrup (page 45)

In a juicer, process the pear, apple, and kale. Transfer to an ice-filled shaker and add lemon juice, vodka, and syrup. Shake the mixture and strain into a martini glass.

✦ ✦ ✦ ✦

SUPERFOOD SPOTLIGHT

One of the most nutrient-dense foods in existence, kale is a cruciferous green vegetable, part of the cabbage family. However, this cocktail will have you saying, "Kale? What kale?"

✦ ✦ ✦ ✦

APPLE BLOSSOM FIZZ

The delicate jasmine adds a lovely dimension to this crisp, green apple whiskey fizz. Top it off with kombucha, a fermented black tea with tremendous health benefits, which will lend a slight carbonation to the final drink. So you can go ahead and get fizzy with it.

1 green apple, juiced
¼ ounce freshly squeezed lemon juice
½ ounce Jasmine Syrup (page 40)
2 ounces whiskey
Splash of kombucha (apple- or ginger-flavored works best)

In an ice-filled shaker, combine all the ingredients, except the kombucha, and shake. Transfer to a glass with fresh ice. Top with the kombucha.

✦ ✦ ✦ ✦

SUPERFOOD SPOTLIGHT

Jasmine is known to eliminate harmful bacteria in the body, as well as ease chronic inflammation, such as muscle aches and pains. Kombucha's health benefits include detoxification, antioxidation, energizing potencies, and promotion of boosting immunity.

✦ ✦ ✦ ✦

TAHITIAN SUNRISE

The zesty citrus, sweet and tart cherries, and Tahitian noni juices in this superfood take on the Tequila Sunrise in a tantalizingly refreshing way.

1 Cherry and Noni Juice Ice Cube (page 31)
2 ounces tequila
4 ounces total freshly squeezed orange, grapefruit, and lime juice

Place one Cherry and Noni Juice Ice Cube at the bottom of a glass, fill the rest of the glass with fresh ice, add the tequila, and top up the glass with the citrus juice. Watch the sunrise.

✦ ✦ ✦ ✦

SUPERFOOD SPOTLIGHT

The immense antioxidant potential of the citrus and cherry juices combined with noni juice's antipsychotic, antifungal, antibacterial, and anti-inflammatory benefits, make this a powerhouse of a drink.

✦ ✦ ✦ ✦

MULE DOWN UNDER

The intensely refreshing eucalyptus adds an unexpected herbal kick to the tropical flair of this kiwi Moscow Mule.

1 kiwi, peeled, plus 1 wheel, for garnish
2 lime wedges, plus 1 wheel, for garnish
½ ounce Eucalyptus Syrup (page 41)
1½ ounces vodka
4 ounces ginger beer

Place the peeled kiwi, lime wedges, and syrup in a shaker and muddle well. Add ice and the vodka and give it a good shake. Double strain into a copper cup filled with fresh ice and top with ginger beer. Garnish with the kiwi and lime wheels.

✦ ✦ ✦ ✦

SUPERFOOD SPOTLIGHT

Eucalyptus, a fast-growing evergreen tree native to Australia with antibacterial, anti-inflammatory, and analgesic properties, has been used for a range of medical conditions in traditional Chinese and Indian medicine. The kiwi has the highest density of any fruit for vitamin C and ranks number one among the top three low-sodium, high-potassium fruits, having more potassium than a banana or citrus fruits.

✦ ✦ ✦ ✦

BLUEBERRY PATCH

The basil and blueberry are a heavenly match in this delightfully refreshing spritzer.

MAKES 6 TO 8 SERVINGS

3 cups blueberries, divided
1 cup freshly squeezed lemon juice
2 cups vodka
1 cup Blueberry Lavender Syrup (page 38)
4 cups soda water (try Fever-Tree sparkling lemon)
Fresh culinary-grade lavender sprigs or Candied Lavender Sprigs
(page 36), for garnish

Freeze 1 cup of the blueberries. Muddle the remaining 2 cups of blueberries, adding the lime juice to the mixture. Shake in an ice-filled shaker, then double strain into a pitcher. Add the vodka and syrup. Add the cup of frozen berries to the pitcher. Pour into six to eight ice-filled glasses and top with soda. Garnish with a sprig of lavender.

✦ ✦ ✦ ✦

SUPERFOOD SPOTLIGHT

Blueberries are an excellent source of manganese, which plays an important part in bone development and converting carbohydrates and fats into energy. These little powerhouses provide tasty ways of staying healthy. Basil's antibacterial and anti-inflammatory qualities will help you fight bacteria, viruses, and chronic illness.

✦ ✦ ✦ ✦

THE PERFECT STORM

The original Dark and Stormy gets a serious kick of fresh ginger and a hint of fresh pear in this variation on the classic drink.

MAKES 6 TO 8 SERVINGS

2 cups dark rum
½ cup freshly squeezed lime juice
½ cup Pear Ginger Syrup (page 45)
3 ounces grated fresh ginger
4 cups ginger beer
Lime wheels, for garnish

Mix the rum, lime juice, syrup, and ginger together in a pitcher. Top with the ginger beer and garnish with lime wheels.

✦ ✦ ✦ ✦

SUPERFOOD SPOTLIGHT

Ginger possesses numerous therapeutic properties, including antioxidant, anti-inflammatory, and detoxifying effects.

✦ ✦ ✦ ✦

THE GOLD RUSH

The vibrant tropical flavor of the pineapple is enhanced by the fragrant cilantro in this unexpected frozen pairing.

2 ounces tequila
1 cup pineapple, cubed and frozen
½ cup coconut water
Garnish with mint leaves and/or pineapple wedge

Place all the ingredients in a blender and blend until smooth. Add ice and blend once more.

✦ ✦ ✦ ✦

SUPERFOOD SPOTLIGHT

Cilantro is a good source of minerals that help control heart rate and blood pressure.

✦ ✦ ✦ ✦

MATCHA JASMINE PEAR POPS

The subtle yet fragrant trio of pear, jasmine, and matcha green tea elevates this poptail to epic flavor proportions.

MAKES 4 POPS

3 tablespoons matcha powder
6 ounces vodka
2 cups cored and chopped ripe pear
1½ cups coconut milk
1 ounce Jasmine Syrup (page 40)

Place all the ingredients in a blender and blend until smooth. Transfer to four Popsicle molds, insert Popsicle sticks, and freeze for 4 to 6 hours.

✦ ✦ ✦ ✦

SUPERFOOD SPOTLIGHT

The metabolism-boosting green tea and the fiber-rich pear boosts energy and vitality, making this refreshing frozen poptail one to come back to.

Z&T TIP

Disposable paper or plastic cups are an easy and inexpensive stand-in for Popsicle molds.

✦ ✦ ✦ ✦

PEACHY MELON

The peach plays up the subtle flavors of the cantaloupe in this bright and refreshing frozen elixir.

2 ounces tequila
¼ cantaloupe, peeled and seeded
2 peaches, pitted
½ ounce Apricot Syrup (page 40)
½ ounce freshly squeezed lime juice

Place all the ingredients in a blender and blend until smooth.

✦ ✦ ✦ ✦

SUPERFOOD SPOTLIGHT

Wonderfully delicious with rich flavor, cantaloupe is rich in numerous health-promoting polyphenolic plant-derived compounds, vitamins, and minerals that are absolute for optimum health.

✦ ✦ ✦ ✦

PINEAPPLE EXPRESS

These cleansing shots are secretly packed with detoxifying wheatgrass powder, but you'll be too busy loving the sweet, tropical pineapple to notice.

MAKES 4 SERVINGS

½ pineapple, peeled
½ lime, peeled
30 mint leaves
1 teaspoon wheatgrass powder
4 ounces tequila

In a juicer, process the pineapple and lime and transfer to a blender. Add the mint, wheatgrass powder, and tequila. Blend well. Pour the mixture into four shot glasses.

✦ ✦ ✦ ✦

SUPERFOOD SPOTLIGHT

This shot, rich in chlorophyll, works to neutralize toxins in the body.

✦ ✦ ✦ ✦

LUCKY CHARM

This little green gem of a shot will have you feeling lucky in no time. The cleansing, nourishing, and ultimately healing properties of the Lucky Charm drink are designed to gently cool your system and leave you feeling refreshed and inspired to take on your day!

MAKES 4 SHOTS

1 green apple
6 kiwis, peeled
1 teaspoon spirulina
4 ounces vodka

In a juicer, process the apple and transfer to a blender. Add the kiwis, spirulina, and vodka. Blend well.

✦ ✦ ✦ ✦

SUPERFOOD SPOTLIGHT

The cleansing, nourishing, and ultimately healing properties of this shot are also designed to gently cool your system and leave you feeling refreshed and inspired to take on your day!
One of the few green fruits, kiwis contain chlorophyll and are rich in vitamin C and carotenoids. Spirulina is considered to be one of nature's most complete foods and is a good source of protein—gram per gram more so than beef, poultry, fish, and soybeans.

✦ ✦ ✦ ✦

CHI CHI CHI CHIA

Clean and simple, this shot will leave you sparkling with pure goodness.

MAKES 4 SHOTS

4 teaspoons chia seeds
4 ounces aloe water
4 ounces Goji Berry Infused Vodka, chilled (page 51)

Stir the chia seeds into the aloe water. Allow the mixture to sit for 10 minutes in the refrigerator to allow the chia seeds to expand and the mixture to chill. Distribute among four shot glasses and top with the chilled vodka. Enjoy.

✦ ✦ ✦ ✦

SUPERFOOD SPOTLIGHT

High in omega-3 fatty acids and packed with protein and fiber, chia seeds can boost energy, lower cholesterol, improve heart health, and stabilize blood sugar.

✦ ✦ ✦ ✦

GARDEN FRESH

The following garden-fresh elixirs are
brimming with earthly green goodness
ready to tantalize your taste buds.

GARDEN VARIETY

This healthy twist on the Bloody Mary is chock-full of fresh market ingredients and a botanical gin.

MAKES 8 SERVINGS

About 10 tomatoes
½ cup watercress
2 green bell peppers
3 celery stalks
1 clove garlic
1 lemon
½ cup fresh parsley
1 teaspoon cayenne pepper
1 cup gin
1 tablespoon Himalayan or sea salt
Freshly ground black pepper

Using a juicer, process the tomatoes, watercress, bell peppers, celery, garlic, lemon, and parsley. Whisk in the cayenne, gin, salt, and black pepper and pour into eight ice-filled glasses. Alternatively, the ingredients can be placed in a blender, blended until smooth, and strained.

✦ ✦ ✦ ✦

Z&T VARIATION

Turn your Bloody Mary into a delicious Michelada, a Mexican beer cocktail, by replacing the gin with your favorite beer.

✦ ✦ ✦ ✦

THE DRUNKEN AVOCADO

The classic tequila and fresh lime juice combo in this green margarita gets an extra delicious kick from the ginger and a smooth texture from the avocado. The pineapple adds just the right tropical sweetness to the mix, while the cilantro complements the overall flavor.

2 tablespoons avocado
1 teaspoon grated fresh ginger
⅓ cup cubed pineapple, plus more for garnish
3 lime wedges
2 cilantro sprigs
2 ounces tequila

In a shaker, muddle the avocado, ginger, pineapple, lime, and cilantro. Fill with ice, add the tequila, and shake well.

Double strain in a glass over ice and garnish with a handful of pineapple cubes.

✦ ✦ ✦ ✦

Z&T TIP

For some extra spice, try dusting your lime wedge in chili powder and rimming your glass with Chili Salt (page 36).

✦ ✦ ✦ ✦

✦ ✦ ✦ ✦

SUPERFOOD SPOTLIGHT

*You'll never know it by taste alone, but this green margarita packs a
serious nutritional punch. This cocktail can reduce inflammation, curb
cardiovascular disease, and smooth digestion.*

✦ ✦ ✦ ✦

THE JESSICA RABBIT

This oregano-infused gin cocktail is elegant and aromatic, making this lovely gin infusion a refreshing choice for brunch.

3 ounces gin
7 oregano sprigs, plus 1 more for garnish
2 ounces freshly juiced carrot juice
1 ounce freshly squeezed grapefruit juice
½ ounce Passion Fruit Syrup (page 46; optional)

Let the oregano infuse in the gin for 24 hours.

Combine all the ingredients, except the reserved oregano sprig, in a shaker with ice and shake vigorously.

Strain the mixture over ice into a cocktail glass and garnish with the reserved oregano sprig.

✦ ✦ ✦ ✦

SUPERFOOD SPOTLIGHT

Oregano is rich in fiber, vitamin K, and omega-3 fatty acids and contains antioxidants that pack a powerful punch. The fresh, crisp carrot juice is a great source of vitamin A, a nutrient that boosts eye and skin health and helps keep the immune system functioning properly. A splash of citrus adds a boost of vitamin C and a refreshing zing.

✦ ✦ ✦ ✦

SERENDIPI-TEA

This green tea martini is reminiscent of a day at the spa. The cucumbers, green tea, and lemongrass play together like a symphony of blissful flavors.

1 cup brewed green tea, chilled
4 cucumbers, peeled, plus more for garnish
1 ounce Lemongrass Syrup (page 43)
4 ounces saké

In a blender, blend the green tea and cucumbers until smooth.

Transfer to an ice-filled shaker. Add the lemongrass syrup and saké. Strain the mixture into a martini glass.

✦ ✦ ✦ ✦

SUPERFOOD SPOTLIGHT

The antioxidants in the green tea and cucumbers work to reduce the formation of free radicals in the body, while the compounds in the lemongrass protect your cells and molecules from damage and aid in their repair.

✦ ✦ ✦ ✦

YELLOW MARY, QUITE CONTRARY

Both the mango and the pineapple add a delightful, tropical sweetness, offsetting the spicy kick of this uniquely flavored yellow Bloody Mary.

MAKES 8 SERVINGS

6 ounces fresh yellow tomato juice
2 ounces yellow bell pepper juice
2 ounces fresh pineapple juice
2 ounces yellow beet juice
2 ounces freshly squeezed lemon juice
2 ounces mango juice
Pinch of white pepper
1 slice of fresh horseradish, or 1 teaspoon prepared
Pinch of salt
Habanero hot sauce
9 ounces vodka
Black Hawaiian salt
8 pineapple wedges, for garnish

Place all the juices and the white pepper, horseradish, salt, and habanero hot sauce to taste in a blender and blend. Transfer to a shaker filled with ice, add the vodka, and shake. Rim eight tall glasses with black Hawaiian salt, fill with ice, and strain the mixture into the glasses. Garnish each with a wedge of pineapple.

SUPERFOOD SPOTLIGHT

Rich in tartaric acid, malic acid, and traces of citric acid, yellow tomatoes help keep the body alkaline.

Z&T TIP

Kick things up a notch by letting fresh, grated horseradish infuse in your spirit for an hour or so.

✦ ✦ ✦ ✦

SECRET GARDEN

This crisp blend of cucumber, grapes, mint, and limeade will keep your thirst quenched and your taste buds happy.

MAKES 6 TO 8 SERVINGS

6 limes
1 cup peeled and chopped cucumber, plus more,
sliced thinly, for serving
⅓ cup Jasmine Syrup (page 40)
3 cups hot water
1 tablespoon chopped fresh lemon balm
1 tablespoon chopped fresh mint
2 cups gin
1 cup grapes, frozen
Mint sprigs, for garnish

Peel the rind off two of the limes. Set the rinds aside. Cut all the limes in half.

In a juicer, process the cup of cucumber and the limes, then strain into a pitcher. Stir in the syrup, hot water, lemon balm, mint, and lime rinds. Let steep on the counter for a minimum of an hour. Strain out the herbs and lime rinds. Allow to cool. Add the gin, thin slices of cucumber, and frozen grapes and garnish with the mint sprigs.

✦ ✦ ✦ ✦

Z&T TIP

Grapes are packed with nutrition and are high in vitamins C and B$_1$, flavonoids, disease-fighting antioxidants, potassium, and manganese.

Not to mention frozen grapes are a treat beyond compare. For best eating, choose a seedless variety. Wash and dry the grapes before placing them on a baking tray lined with wax paper, and place in the freezer for about an hour. The frozen grapes won't water down your drink or cool it down too quickly like ice cubes would. Plus, you have a delicious snack waiting for you at the bottom of the glass!

✦ ✦ ✦ ✦

HONEYDEW PUNCH

Let this honey-sweet, honeydew melon punch, with mint and basil, shine at your next party.

MAKES 6 TO 8 SERVINGS

1 honeydew melon, quartered, peeled, and seeded, divided
½ cup Lemongrass Syrup (page 43)
1 cup aloe water
¼ cup packed fresh mint
¼ cup fresh basil
½ cup freshly squeezed lime juice
2 cups tequila
Mint sprigs, for garnish
Lime wedges, for garnish

Cut three of the melon quarters into 1-inch chunks. Purée in a food processor until smooth. Strain the purée through a cheesecloth-lined sieve, and discard the solids. (You should have about 4 cups.) Using a 1-inch melon baller, scoop balls from remaining melon quarter, and reserve.

Combine the melon purée, syrup, aloe water, mint, basil, and lime juice in a pitcher and refrigerate until cold, about 30 minutes. Add the tequila and ice to a pitcher, and divide among six to eight glasses. Garnish each with melon balls, mint sprigs, and lime wedges, and serve immediately.

Z&T TIP

Guess what? You can freeze your melon balls to keep your pitcher perfect drink cool without watering it down with ice cubes. Simply place the melon balls on a baking tray and freeze. Alternatively, if you don't want to go through the trouble of making melon balls, consider puréeing your melon in a blender and transferring the contents into ice cube trays to freeze!

✦ ✦ ✦ ✦

MARIA VERDE

Make this fun, lively, green Bloody Mary with tomatillos and tequila and you'll be the hit of your next fiesta. The original Bloody Mary is traditionally assumed to have been invented by George Jessel, and then perfected by Fernand Petiot, who first added spices to what was originally just vodka and tomato juice. The drink was then known as the "Red Snapper."

MAKES 12 SERVINGS

12 ounces tequila
16 ounces tomatillo juice
3 ounces green bell pepper juice
3 ounces cucumber juice
3 ounces celery juice
3 ounces freshly squeezed lime juice
½ teaspoon salt
½ teaspoon celery salt
½ teaspoon freshly ground white pepper
1 teaspoon grated fresh horseradish
½ jalapeño pepper, or more to taste
12 long slices cucumber

Place all the ingredients in a blender and blend until smooth. Transfer to a pitcher. Refrigerate for 2 hours. Pour into 12 long glasses over ice. Garnish each with a cucumber slice.

ZESTY CUCUMBER MARGARITA

Cooling and remarkably refreshing, this frozen twist on the classic margarita, upgraded with the mineral-packed cucumber and frozen on a stick, will make you swoon.

MAKES 6 POPS

6 ounces tequila
2 cups cucumber (peeled if not organic)
½ cup freshly squeezed lime juice
½ cup Rosemary Sage Syrup (page 47)
1 cup coconut water

Place all the ingredients in a blender and blend until smooth. Pour into six Popsicle molds, insert Popsicle sticks, and freeze for a minimum of 4 hours.

❖ ❖ ❖ ❖

Z&T TIP

The most important part of freezing alcohol is mastering the proportion. If you add too much alcohol, your pops will not freeze correctly and you'll be left with a slushy mess. Use a 4:1 ratio of mixer to alcohol so they freeze just right. Now go forth and create!

❖ ❖ ❖ ❖

SANGRITA

Sangrita, meaning "little blood," is a classic savory accompaniment to a good sipping tequila. Traditionally made with Seville oranges, pomegranate juice, and spices, it is sometimes mistakenly made with tomatoes and spices as well. As with most recipes in the book, you can have this as a nonalcoholic drink, combine it with the tequila for a delicious, nutritious shooter, or sip it, in traditional style, alongside a tequila of your choosing.

MAKES 4 SHOTS

8 tomatoes
4 celery stalks
1 lime
4 ounces tequila
Pinch of cayenne pepper
Pinch of sea salt

In a juicer, process the tomatoes, celery, and lime. Combine with the remaining ingredients in a shaker with ice and strain into four shot glasses.

✦ ✦ ✦ ✦

SUPERFOOD SPOTLIGHT

As an excellent source of strong antioxidants, tomatoes can help combat the formation of free radicals known to cause diseases, while celery is among the best natural sources of hydrating electrolytes. Together, this duo makes this savory shot a nutritional powerhouse.

✦ ✦ ✦ ✦

GLOW, BABY, GLOW

This cucumber honeydew kale shot works to purify your skin from the inside out. Drink and glow.

MAKES 4 SHOTS

4 large kale leaves
1 apple
½ honeydew melon
1 medium-size cucumber
1 lime
4 ounces gin

Juice all the ingredients, except the gin. Transfer to a shaker with ice and add the gin. Pour into four shot glasses.

✦ ✦ ✦ ✦

SUPERFOOD SPOTLIGHT

Did you know that kale contains more calcium per calorie than milk? Kale also has more iron than beef, and with its 3:1 ratio of carbohydrate to protein, its nutritional density is unparalleled among green leafy vegetables.

✦ ✦ ✦ ✦

PEAR AND PARSLEY BOOSTER

This vibrant green shot keeps your immune system strong, tones your bones, and heals the nervous system. It helps flush excess fluid from the body, thus supporting kidney function as well.

MAKES 4 SHOTS

2 ripe pears
2 apples
Handful of parsley
4 ounces vodka
Pear Ginger Syrup (page 45)

Juice all the ingredients, except the vodka and syrup. In a shaker with ice, mix well with the vodka. Adjust the sweetness to taste, using the syrup. Pair with vodka, tequila, or gin.

✦ ✦ ✦ ✦

SUPERFOOD SPOTLIGHT

Parsley is an anti-inflammatory and antiseptic herb helpful in keeping the bladder and kidneys in good health. The leaves and the roots of the herb are also beneficial for the maintenance of the spleen and the liver.

✦ ✦ ✦ ✦

HOT GREENS

Get your calcium needs met while you tantalize your mouth with this cleansing, spicy green beauty.

MAKES 4 SHOTS

2 cucumbers
4 celery stalks
3 kale leaves
1 bunch cilantro
1 jalapeño pepper, seeds partially or entirely removed,
depending on your hotness preference
½ lime
4 ounces tequila

Juice all the ingredients, except the tequila. In a shaker with ice, mix well with the tequila. This juice pairs very well with tequila, but vodka or gin work as well.

✦ ✦ ✦ ✦

SUPERFOOD SPOTLIGHT

Cilantro is rich with an unusual array of healing phytonutrients and antioxidants. It is antiseptic, analgesic, and aphrodisiac. It's also most powerful in its raw state or juiced form. Additionally, cilantro is one of the few herbs that can help remove heavy metals from the body.

✦ ✦ ✦ ✦

FLORAL AND FRAGRANT

These soothing aromatic sips are as inviting as they are fragrant.

SPICED HIBISCUS TEA

This tart, fragrant, vibrantly colored tea is extremely refreshing in the summer months; however, the added cinnamon and ginger both create a warmth in the body that promotes circulation especially vital in the cold months as well.

MAKES 2 SERVINGS

2 teaspoons dried culinary-grade hibiscus flowers
1 (½-inch) piece fresh ginger, finely chopped
½ cinnamon stick
4 ounces pomegranate juice
2 cups water
¾ ounce Raspberry Rose Syrup (page 44)
3 ounces vodka
Orange slices

Place the hibiscus flowers, ginger, and cinnamon stick in a large pan with the pomegranate juice and water. Bring slowly to a boil and simmer for 2 minutes.

Turn off the heat and allow the mixture to infuse for 5 minutes. Strain through a sieve and pour into two tall glasses. Add the syrup and vodka. Serve warm with the orange slices.

✦ ✦ ✦ ✦

SUPERFOOD SPOTLIGHT

Hibiscus packs a bounty of healthful properties. Rich in vitamin C, it has been used widely as an herbal method for controlling high blood pressure, tempering fevers, alleviating digestive problems, and improving circulatory disorders.

✦ ✦ ✦ ✦

MULLED MYSTIC

The first documented roots of mulled wine stem back as far as Ancient Egypt, when spiced wine was used for medicinal purposes and was considered to be a remedial elixir of the afterlife.

This traditional drink served over the holidays gets a modern makeover here. The oftentimes heavily mulled drink is lightened and brightened by switching out the red wine for a lighter white one. The addition of citrus, ginger, and vanilla notes also serves to warm yet uplift. Finally, the pomegranate seeds brighten up this delightful sipper further yet by increasing its medicinal value.

MAKES ABOUT 1 QUART

3 whole cloves
Zest from 1 small lemon, removed in strips with a vegetable peeler
1 (2-inch) piece fresh peeled ginger
½ vanilla bean, halved lengthwise and seeds scraped out
1 (750 ml) bottle medium-bodied dry or off-dry white wine
1 cup Goji Berry Infused Vodka (page 51)
½ cup Pear Ginger Syrup (page 45)
Lemon twists, for garnish
Pomegranate seeds, for garnish

Stick the cloves into two or three strips of the lemon zest. In a medium-size nonreactive saucepan over medium heat, combine the ginger, vanilla bean (pod and seeds), and about two-thirds of the lemon zest strips (including the clove-studded pieces) and cover partially. Simmer, stirring occasionally, until fragrant and thickened slightly, about 5 minutes. Add the wine, cover partially, and simmer until the wine is infused, at least 1 hour (do not allow to boil). Remove and discard the ginger, vanilla bean pod, cloves, and lemon zest. Add the infused vodka and syrup. Serve in a wineglass or brandy snifter, garnished with lemon twists and pomegranate seeds.

HOT PASSION TODDY

Elevate the classic hot toddy with the addition of the bright and cheery goji berries and the delightful passion fruit syrup.

1 cup water
1 tablespoon goji berries
½ ounce freshly squeezed lemon juice
½ ounce Passion Fruit Syrup (page 46)
1½ ounces rum

Bring the water to boil and pour over the goji berries. Let the berries soak for at least an hour to plump up. Transfer the mixture to a pot, add the lemon juice, and simmer for a few minutes.

Pour into a glass, add the syrup, and top off with the rum. The plumped goji berries are a delicious treat at the bottom of the glass.

✦ ✦ ✦ ✦

SUPERFOOD SPOTLIGHT

Unique among all fruits, the goji berry contains all essential amino acids, has the highest concentration of protein of any fruit, and is loaded with vitamin C. There is no doubt that the humble goji berry is a nutritional powerhouse.

✦ ✦ ✦ ✦

AMBROSIA

The unassuming chamomile, paired with lemon and enhanced with the sweet and aromatic apricot syrup, creates a lovely, soothing libation to be enjoyed both hot and cold.

4 ounces freshly brewed chamomile tea
½ ounce Apricot Syrup (page 40)
½ ounce freshly squeezed lemon juice
2 ounces gin
Orange twist, for garnish

Add the syrup and lemon juice to a mug of the hot tea, then add the gin. Garnish with an orange twist.

✦ ✦ ✦ ✦

SUPERFOOD SPOTLIGHT

Chamomile actually has quite a medicinal history. The plant has been used for centuries in teas as a mild, relaxing sleep aid; a treatment for fevers, colds, and stomach ailments; and an anti-inflammatory.

✦ ✦ ✦ ✦

GYPSY ROSE SIPPER

The subtle yet distinctive aroma of the cardamom, the native spice to the evergreen forests of India, with its peppery, citrusy warmth, makes this sipper with rose syrup an invitingly simple yet elegant one.
MAKES 2 SERVINGS

2 cups water
2 crushed cardamom pods
2 lemon peels
2 orange peels
1 ounce Raspberry Rose Syrup (page 44)
3 ounces rum
Mint sprigs, for garnish

In a medium-size saucepan, bring the water, cardamom pods, and lemon and orange peels to a boil. Add the rose syrup and rum. Serve with fresh mint sprigs.

✦ ✦ ✦ ✦

SUPERFOOD SPOTLIGHT

Cardamom has been used in Ayurvedic medicine as a treatment for mouth ulcers, digestive problems, and even depression. It is a wonderful detoxifier, anti-inflammatory, and powerful antioxidant.

✦ ✦ ✦ ✦

LADY GREY

Tea lovers, rejoice. This elegant drink, made with lavender honey syrup, plays up the flavors of the tea in a delicate and aromatic way.

1½ ounces vodka
4 ounces brewed Earl Grey tea, chilled
¾ ounce Blueberry Lavender Syrup (page 38)
1 large Almond Milk and Vanilla Ice Cube (page 31)
1 culinary-grade lavender sprig or Candied Lavender Sprig
(page 36)

Place all of the ingredients, except the ice cube and lavender sprig, in a cocktail shaker with ice. Shake several times. Then strain the cocktail into a glass over the flavored ice cube. Garnish with the lavender sprig.

✦ ✦ ✦ ✦

SUPERFOOD SPOTLIGHT

There are many medicinal properties associated with lavender. The soothing herb is most often used to calm your stomach, mind, and skin.

✦ ✦ ✦ ✦

ZEN AND TONIC

Infusing the gin with rosebud tea adds a relaxed sophistication to the classic G&T, while a splash of aloe water and a touch of lavender increases its medicinal qualities. Add a splash of elderflower tonic to top off this Zen and Tonic.

2 ounces Rose Infused Gin (page 52)
½ ounce Blueberry Lavender Syrup (page 38)
½ ounce aloe water
4 ounces elderflower tonic water

In a shaker with ice, combine the infused gin, syrup, and aloe water and shake well. Strain into a glass with fresh ice and top off with the elderflower tonic water.

✦ ✦ ✦ ✦

SUPERFOOD SPOTLIGHT

Rose petal tea has been prescribed as part of Chinese medicine for more than 5,000 years to ease depression, soothe the nerves, increase circulation, and reduce indigestion.

✦ ✦ ✦ ✦

SECRETS OF A GEISHA

Plums and rose tea create a delicate drink that complements the plum wine and saké fabulously.

1½ ounces plums
2 ounces brewed rosebud tea, chilled
¾ ounce Raspberry Rose Syrup (page 44)
2 ounces saké
1 ounce plum wine

In a juicer, process the plums.

In a shaker with ice, combine the plums, chilled rosebud tea, syrup, saké, and plum wine. Shake and strain into a martini glass or coupe.

✦ ✦ ✦ ✦

SUPERFOOD SPOTLIGHT

Plums help increase iron absorption in the body and work to regulate blood sugar levels.

✦ ✦ ✦ ✦

THE BLUSHING ROSE SANGRIA

This delicate take on sangria spotlights the strawberry and the rose in perfect unison.

MAKES 8 TO 10 SERVINGS

2 cups strawberries
1 cup culinary-grade rose petals
2 ounces rose water
1 (750 ml) bottle rosé wine
1 (750 ml) bottle sparkling wine

Combine the strawberries, rose petals, rose water, and rosé wine in a large pitcher.

Stir together, then let sit for at least 4 hours (or overnight) so that the flavors can infuse.

Just before serving, pour in the sparkling wine and stir.

✦ ✦ ✦ ✦

SUPERFOOD SPOTLIGHT

If you're not already a fan of strawberries, you should be! Not only are they juicy, summery, and delicious, their impact on the reduction of LDL, inflammation, and high blood pressure earns strawberries the title of one of the heart-healthiest fruits you can eat.

✦ ✦ ✦ ✦

BOURBON PEACH SWEET TEA

Prepare to stimulate your senses with this peach–infused sweet tea. With fragrant jasmine, citrus, and mint notes, this is the perfect porch-sipping, summer-heat-beating cocktail around.

MAKES 6 TO 8 SERVINGS

2 peaches
2 cups bourbon
6 cups water
4 black tea bags
¼ cup Jasmine Syrup (page 40)
6 sliced orange rounds
6 mint sprigs

To make the bourbon-soaked peaches:

Submerge whole peaches in boiling water for 1 minute. Transfer to an ice bath to stop the cooking process. The skin will slip right off! Cut the peaches into wedges and place in a mason jar or comparable container.

Pour the bourbon over the peaches and secure the lid tightly. Store in a dark, cool place for up to 1 week.

For the tea:

Bring the water to a boil. Turn off the heat and add the tea bags. Steep the tea for 3 to 5 minutes. Remove the tea bags, transfer the tea to a large pitcher, and let rest in the refrigerator until cold.

Place the Jasmine Syrup, orange slices, and mint in a medium-size bowl and muddle. Once the mixture is pressed together and the flavors are extracted, add the bourbon to the mixture and strain into the pitcher of tea. Stir well. Add the bourbon-soaked peaches to the tea.

Fill six to eight glasses with ice cubes. Pour the sweet, boozy tea over the ice. Enjoy

✦ ✦ ✦ ✦

SUPERFOOD SPOTLIGHT

Did you know that stone fruits like peaches, plums, and nectarines have been shown to ward off obesity-related diseases such as diabetes, metabolic syndromes, and cardiovascular disease? Reason enough to enjoy these gems more often!

✦ ✦ ✦ ✦

LAVENDER LEMONADE

This beautiful, refreshing drink is a fusion of lavender, blueberries, and good old-fashioned lemonade. This treat can be sipped on a hot summer day, to give a lift to all your senses.

MAKES 6 TO 8 SERVINGS

6 lemons
3 cups blueberries
1 cup aloe water
½ cup Blueberry Lavender Syrup (page 38)
2 cups vodka
3 cups seltzer or elderflower soda

Process the lemons and blueberries in a juicer. Transfer to a punch bowl and stir in the aloe water and syrup, then top with the vodka and soda.

✦ ✦ ✦ ✦

SUPERFOOD SPOTLIGHT

Aloe vera's active ingredients are sulfur, lupeol, salicylic acid, cinnamic acid, urea nitrogen, and phenol, which are substances that prevent the growth of disease-causing micro-organisms and help to treat fungal and viral infections. Aloe vera contains over 200 active components including vitamins, minerals, amino acids, enzymes, polysaccharide, and fatty acids and has been used therapeutically for over 5,000 years—now that's a long-standing track record!

✦ ✦ ✦ ✦

SUMMER BLOSSOM

A medley of fruit and flowers will help you celebrate the season's finest.

MAKES 6 TO 8 SERVINGS

¼ cup culinary-grade marigold petals
1 tablespoon dried culinary-grade rosebuds
1 tablespoon dried culinary-grade lavender buds
1 tablespoon grated orange zest
4 cups boiling water
⅓ cup Orange Marigold Syrup (page 42)
3 peaches, pitted and cubed
3 apricots, pitted and cubed
3 oranges, sliced
1 cup coconut water
1 (750 ml) bottle white wine
1 (750 ml) bottle sparkling wine
Whole, culinary-grade flowers, for garnish

Place the marigold petals, rosebuds, lavender buds, and orange zest in a teapot and fill with the boiling water. Steep for 5 minutes. Strain the tea into a pitcher and discard the solids. Add the syrup and stir to dissolve. Chill.

Combine the fruit, tea, coconut water, and white wine in a pitcher. Stir in the sparkling wine and garnish with whole flowers.

BLUEBERRY LILAC GRANITA

Blueberries' natural sweetness help create this full-flavored, elegant floral granita with minimum effort.

MAKES 1 PINT

¾ cup vodka
3 cups blueberries
⅔ cup freshly squeezed lemon juice
½ cup Lilac Syrup (page 40)

Place all the ingredients in a blender and blend until frosty and smooth. Transfer the mixture to a shallow container and freeze for 1 hour. Remove from the freezer, stir to create slush, and return to the freezer for another 2 hours. To serve, scrape the surface with a spoon and transfer the granita to serving glasses.

✦ ✦ ✦ ✦

SUPERFOOD SPOTLIGHT

The edible lilac flower has a history of medicinal use. Lilacs are effective at eliminating intestinal parasites, and were often used in the treatment of malaria. They also aid in reducing fever.

✦ ✦ ✦ ✦

SWEET AND SPICY

Prepare to stimulate your taste buds with these zesty, vibrant flavor combinations.

DRAGON KISS

The fiery hot jalapeño pairs well with the sweet, tart, antioxidant-rich ruby red cherry in this unmistakably warming drink.

1 slice jalapeño, plus more for garnish
2 ounces tequila
1 cup fresh cherries, juiced

Muddle the jalapeño slice at the bottom of a cup or shaker, add the tequila, and mix. Place a large ice cube in a glass and slowly strain the mixture over the ice. Top with the cherry juice. Garnish with additional jalapeño.

✦ ✦ ✦ ✦

SUPERFOOD SPOTLIGHT

One cup of cherries has about the same amount of potassium found in a small banana, which helps keep blood pressure in check. Cherries also contain good amounts of the antioxidants quercetin and anthocyanin, which help protect against cancer and cardiovascular disease.

✦ ✦ ✦ ✦

LIQUID GOLD

The tart sweetness of the tropical pineapple pairs remarkably well with winter spices, making the warmth and aroma of this drink one that will make you forget all about the snow outside.

2 teaspoons total whole allspice berries, black peppercorns, and whole cloves
½ cinnamon stick
1 cup juiced pineapple
¼ vanilla bean pod, split in half lengthwise, seeds scraped out
¼ cup cubed pineapple
Ground cinnamon
2 ounces dark rum

Preheat the oven to 350°F.

Place the allspice, peppercorns, cloves, and cinnamon stick in a medium-size saucepan. Stir over medium heat until fragrant, about 2 minutes. Add the juiced pineapple and vanilla bean and seeds and bring to a simmer over medium heat, stirring occasionally. Lower the heat to the lowest setting and simmer for 15 minutes.

While the pot simmers, sprinkle the pineapple cubes with cinnamon and roast in the oven for the remaining time.

Strain the mixture through a fine-mesh sieve and discard the solids. To serve, place the pineapple chunks in a cup, pour in the rum and ladle in the spiced juice.

✦ ✦ ✦ ✦

SUPERFOOD SPOTLIGHT

Fresh pineapple is the only known source of an enzyme called bromelain, which helps in alleviating joint pain and arthritis, and reducing inflammation.

✦ ✦ ✦ ✦

FINE AND SHANDY

This sweet and spicy beer cocktail with apricot syrup and serrano chiles may be the perfect summer beverage.

¼ cup organic lemon soda
1 tablespoon Apricot Syrup (page 40)
1 thin slice serrano chile
6 ounces pale ale or lager, chilled

In a tall, ice-filled glass, combine the soda, syrup, and chile slice. Top with the chilled beer.

✦ ✦ ✦ ✦

Z&T TIP
For extra heat, muddle the chile to release more spice.

✦ ✦ ✦ ✦

FAR EAST

This frozen lychee martini is on fire. Enjoy the beautiful pairing of sweet lychees and spicy Thai chile pepper. In Ancient China, lychees were the favored fruit in the imperial corridors, finding their greatest fans amongst the kings and queens who would get these beautiful fruits transported to the capital at a great cost to the kingdom.

2 ounces saké
6 lychees, peeled and seeded
1 Thai chile
½ ounce Lemongrass Syrup (page 43)
Juice of 2 limes

Place all the ingredients in a blender and blend until puréed. Add ice and blend until smooth.

✦ ✦ ✦ ✦

SUPERFOOD SPOTLIGHT

Immensely alkaline, the mineral composition of lychees also keeps our blood count healthy.

✦ ✦ ✦ ✦

FIERY MANGO POPS

The sweet tropical mango paired with a hint of heat in this frozen pop will stimulate and delight. Best yet, the duo masks the incredibly potent secret ingredient: turmeric, which boasts major anti-inflammatory properties.

MAKES 4 POPS

6 ounces rum
2½ cups frozen mango chunks
1 (½-inch-long) red jalapeño pepper
1 teaspoon ground turmeric, or 1 (½-inch piece) fresh turmeric root
Juice of 1 orange
2 tablespoons freshly squeezed lime juice

Place all the ingredients in a blender and blend until smooth. Add ice and blend once more. Pour into four Popsicle molds, add Popsicle sticks, and freeze for 4 hours.

✦ ✦ ✦ ✦

Z&T TIP

By using frozen fruit, you can use less ice, which will assure your drink is rich in flavor.

✦ ✦ ✦ ✦

GINGER SNAP

This naturally sweet shot with just a kick of ginger will help regulate your blood sugar levels and keep you alkaline.

MAKES 4 SERVINGS

4 apples
6 carrots
1 (1-inch) piece fresh ginger
4 ounces rum

In a juicer, process the apples, carrots, and ginger, transfer to a shaker with ice, and add the rum. Pour into four shot glasses.

✦ ✦ ✦ ✦

SUPERFOOD SPOTLIGHT

The medicinal uses of ginger have been known for at least 2,000 years in cultures all around the world. Ginger has broad-spectrum antibacterial, antiviral, antioxidant, and anti-parasitic properties that help reduce inflammation, making it valuable for relief of joint pain, menstrual pain, headaches, and more.

✦ ✦ ✦ ✦

PEACH HONEY BOMB

Luscious, sweet peaches reign supreme in this powerful little shot.

4 ounces whiskey
2 peaches, pitted
Juice of 1 lemon
1 tablespoon honey
1 teaspoon ground turmeric

Place all the ingredients in a blender and blend well. Serve chilled.

✦ ✦ ✦ ✦

SUPERFOOD SPOTLIGHT

Turmeric, the bright orange spice, has long been used in the Chinese and Indian systems of medicine as an anti-inflammatory agent to treat a wide variety of conditions.

✦ ✦ ✦ ✦

THE RETOX
DETOX

Detox while you retox with this purifying grapefruit, cayenne, and maple shot.

MAKES 4 SERVINGS

2 pink grapefruits, peeled
1 teaspoon pure maple syrup
½ teaspoon cayenne pepper
4 ounces vodka

In a juicer, process the grapefruits and mix with the maple syrup and cayenne. Transfer to a blender and blend until the syrup has dissolved. Add the vodka and pour into four shot glasses.

✦ ✦ ✦ ✦

Z&T VARIATION

This can also be enjoyed as a cocktail or as a cleansing, detoxing juice.

✦ ✦ ✦ ✦

THE MEXICAN CHOCOLATE BUZZ

This delicious shot made with raw cacao and chili promotes detoxification.

MAKES 4 SHOTS

4 ounces tequila
1 cup coconut water
1 tablespoon cacao powder
2 tablespoons pure maple syrup, or more if desired
1 teaspoon pure vanilla extract
½ teaspoon chili powder

Place all the ingredients in a blender and blend well. Sweeten to your liking with more maple syrup, if you wish, and pour into four shot glasses. Pairs well with tequila, rum, and even bourbon.

✦ ✦ ✦ ✦

SUPERFOOD SPOTLIGHT

Cacao is very rich in magnesium, an important mineral, aiding in the absorption of calcium and promoting detoxification.

✦ ✦ ✦ ✦

RICH AND CREAMY

These harmonious concoctions with rich, creamy notes will have you swooning with delight.

HOMEMADE NUT MILK

Simply blended with water, many types of nuts and seeds transform into a creamy dairy alternative. You can purchase a variety of nut milks at most food stores these days, yet making them at home is a fresher, healthier, and less expensive alternative. Best of all, it's a simple process!

MAKES 3 TO 4 CUPS

1 cup raw almonds, hazelnuts, pistachios, pecans, walnuts,
cashews, or peanuts
Filtered water, enough to cover nuts by 2 inches
4 cups very hot water, plus more as needed

Place the nuts in a large bowl and add water to cover by 2 inches. Let stand for at least 12 hours. The longer the nuts soak, the smoother the milk will be.

Drain the nuts; discard the soaking liquid. Purée the nuts and 4 cups of very hot water (hot water yields a creamier milk) in a blender on high speed until very smooth, about 2 minutes. Strain through a fine-mesh sieve into a medium-size bowl, pressing down on the solids.

Discard the nut pulp. Thin the nut milk with water as necessary to reach your desired consistency. Transfer to an airtight container and chill until cold.

✦ ✦ ✦ ✦

Z&T VARIATION

For a sweeter milk, blend in a pitted date or two. For flavored milks, add cinnamon, vanilla, or cacao.

✦ ✦ ✦ ✦

CARAMELIZED BANANA

This creamy dessertlike frozen drink with bourbon features sweet caramelized bananas.

MAKES 2 SERVINGS

2 bananas, peeled and sliced into rounds
1 tablespoon pure maple syrup
1 tablespoon coconut oil
4 ounces bourbon
1 cup almond milk

In a medium-size bowl, coat the bananas in maple syrup and toss. Heat the coconut oil in a pan over medium heat and add the banana. Cook for 5 minutes, flipping occasionally until the banana has browned and the sugar has caramelized. Remove from the heat and transfer back to the bowl. Pour the bourbon over the bananas and let soak for 15 minutes. Place the bowl in the freezer for an additional 10 minutes. Remove the banana mixture from the freezer, combine in a blender with the almond milk and ice, and blend.

✦ ✦ ✦ ✦

Z&T TIP

To keep this drink creamy in consistency, avoid over-blending. Begin on the lowest setting and build up the speed on your blender gradually

✦ ✦ ✦ ✦

GOLDEN MILK PUNCH

This may very well be the perfect comfort drink to be enjoyed curled up on the couch on a cold winter's day. Yet I've enjoyed it just as often in a tall glass over ice. However you choose to serve it, feel good knowing the warming spices and the peppery turmeric's potent anti-inflammatory benefits are helping you boost your immunity.

MAKES 2 SERVINGS

2 cups coconut milk
¼ ounce pure vanilla extract
¾ ounce pure maple syrup
Freshly grated nutmeg
Ground cinnamon
½ teaspoon ground turmeric
3 ounces rum

In a medium-size saucepan, combine the coconut milk, vanilla, maple syrup, a pinch each of nutmeg and cinnamon, and turmeric over medium-low heat. Stir constantly, being careful not to burn the milk. Bring almost to a boil and remove from heat.

Divide between two mugs and add 1½ ounces of rum to each mug. Serve sprinkled with freshly grated nutmeg and a pinch of cinnamon.

✦ ✦ ✦ ✦

SUPERFOOD SPOTLIGHT

Turmeric has long been used in the Chinese and Indian systems of medicine as an anti-inflammatory agent to treat a wide variety of conditions, including hemorrhage, toothache, bruises, chest pain, and colic. It is also what gives this milk punch its golden hue.

✦ ✦ ✦ ✦

BOOZY BOURBON CHAI

Made from some of the world's most medicinally active herbs, the sweet, spicy, and pungent chai tea has an impressive list of ingredients with their own powerful health benefits, yet I boost their power further by adding the earthy chaga mushroom to the mix.

MAKES 2 SERVINGS

8 ounces almond milk
½ teaspoon ground chaga
½ cinnamon stick
2 cardamom pods, crushed
1 (½-inch) piece fresh ginger
¼ ounce pure vanilla extract, or 1 vanilla bean
1 tablespoon coconut sugar
2 sachets organic whole red rooibos tea
3 ounces bourbon

Combine the almond milk, chaga, spices, vanilla, and coconut sugar in a small saucepan. Bring to a boil and simmer for 8 minutes, stirring occasionally. Remove from the heat. Add the tea sachet and steep for 5 minutes. Remove the sachet, strain out the spices, and pour into a warmed cup. Add the bourbon. Sit back and enjoy.

✦ ✦ ✦ ✦

SUPERFOOD SPOTLIGHT

The synergy creates a potent tonic that helps support digestion, lower blood sugar, and promote cardiovascular health.

✦ ✦ ✦ ✦

HARD NOG LIFE

Did you know that George Washington was a fan of eggnog? Kitchen records at Mount Vernon reveal that the former President served the drink to his guests quite frequently. His version of the drink included rye whiskey, rum, and sherry.

MAKES 2 SERVINGS

1 cup plain almond milk
1 cup canned light coconut milk
2 tablespoons pure maple syrup
4 teaspoons pure vanilla extract
¼ teaspoon freshly grated nutmeg
Pinch of salt
3 ounces rum

Combine all the ingredients, except the rum, in a medium-size saucepan and place over medium heat. Bring to a boil, then lower the heat to a simmer while whisking continuously. Continue to whisk while the liquid simmers for 4 minutes. Remove from the heat and pour carefully into a heatproof jar on the counter to cool, uncovered. Once cooled, place in an airtight jar in the refrigerator to chill and set for at least 4 hours before serving. Once ready, pour into two cups and top with the rum.

HARVEST MOON

All the quintessential fall flavors in one unique presentation. This is your new autumn sipper.

Cinnamon Sugar
3 ounces whiskey
1 ounce Pear Ginger Syrup (page 45)
Splash of freshly squeezed orange juice
2 tablespoons pure organic pumpkin purée
2 ounces kombucha
Orange twist

Rim a glass with Cinnamon Sugar (see page 35). Mix the whiskey, syrup, orange juice, and pumpkin purée. Top with the kombucha. Garnish with an orange twist.

✦ ✦ ✦ ✦

SUPERFOOD SPOTLIGHT

The pumpkin purée in this recipe is a top source of beta-carotene, a powerful antioxidant that gives orange vegetables and fruits their vibrant color and which is converted to vitamin A in the body. Pumpkins also help protect against disease, and delay aging and body degeneration. Here's to fall harvest!

✦ ✦ ✦ ✦

BOOZY HOT CHOCOLATE

What is more comforting than a cup of hot chocolate? Well, your comfort level can spike up tenfold, knowing that the nutrients found in raw cacao improve circulation, promote cardiovascular health, neutralize free radicals in the body, and enhance physical and mental well-being. Now, that calls for a celebratory cup!

MAKES 2 SERVINGS

2 cups almond milk
1 tablespoon raw cacao powder
½ teaspoon ground cinnamon
1 orange peel
2 teaspoons pure maple syrup
1 teaspoon pure vanilla extract
3 ounces orange vodka

Combine the almond milk, cacao, cinnamon, orange peel, maple syrup, and vanilla in a small pot. Heat gently while stirring. Pour into two cups, add the orange vodka, and enjoy.

✦ ✦ ✦ ✦

Z&T TIP

Cacao is often confused with cocoa powder. Cocoa is the processed form of cacao, which lessens its nutritional value, especially when it comes to antioxidants. If you are unable to find pure cacao, choose a cocoa powder without added fillers or sugars.

✦ ✦ ✦ ✦

WARM CINNAMON HORCHATA

Traditional Mexican horchata is made with rice, milk, cinnamon, and lots of sugar. This new version is endlessly creamy, yet is uniquely dairy free. Instead, we're using soaked cashews and a handful of Medjool dates, for a caramel-like sweetness.

MAKES 4 SERVINGS

⅓ cup uncooked white rice
¼ cup raw cashews
1 teaspoon vanilla extract
3 cups water
1 teaspoon ground cinnamon, plus more for garnish
5 Medjool dates and/or pure maple syrup
6 ounces rum

Soak the rice and cashews together in several inches of water for 2 to 6 hours, until softened. Drain off the soaking water and combine the rice and cashews in a blender with the vanilla, water, cinnamon, and dates. If the dates don't provide enough sweetness, feel free to add some maple syrup. Blend on high speed for 2 minutes to purée all ingredients. Strain, using a cheesecloth. Pour into four glasses and top with the rum. Sprinkle more cinnamon on top.

BLISS

Take a trip down bliss lane with this heavenly rich and creamy concoction.

1 teaspoon matcha powder
1 cup hot water
1 teaspoon coconut sugar
3 ounces coconut milk
4 ounces saké
Dried unsweetened shredded coconut

Spoon the matcha into a large mug. Add the hot water, coconut sugar, and coconut milk and use a matcha whisk to whisk briskly, in an up-and-down motion, until frothy, about 30 seconds. Alternatively, you can use a small kitchen whisk if you don't have a matcha whisk.

Transfer the mixture to shaker with ice, add the saké, and shake. Rim a glass with the coconut flakes, fill with ice, and strain the contents of the shaker into the glass.

✦ ✦ ✦ ✦

SUPERFOOD SPOTLIGHT

If you haven't heard of matcha yet, it is time to get acquainted with this milky green, metabolism-enhancing, stress-reducing, immune-boosting, cholesterol-lowering wonder of a tea. One cup of matcha green tea has as many antioxidants as 10 cups of regular tea and is the tea of choice of Zen Buddhist monks, who drink it to remain alert and calm during long hours of meditation.

✦ ✦ ✦ ✦

A DASH AND A WINK

Bold is the name of the game in this robust, flavorful elixir. The blackstrap molasses bonds well with the coffee for a rich, robust taste.

MAKES 6 TO 8 CUPS

Cold-brew coffee:
1 cup coarsely ground coffee beans
4 cups cold water

Per serving:
4 ounces cold-brew coffee
8 to 12 ounces water
1 to 2 teaspoons blackstrap molasses
2 ounces Vanilla Infused Rum (page 54)
Almond Milk and Vanilla Ice Cubes (page 31)

To cold-brew the coffee, place the ground coffee and cold water together in a large bowl. Stir briefly to combine. Cover, and refrigerate for at least 12 hours (or up to 24 hours).

Place a strainer covered with a cheesecloth atop a second bowl. Pour the coffee (and grounds) through the strainer and wait a minute or two until the liquid has filtered through the strainer. Discard the grounds.

Serve the coffee over ice, stirring in water to dilute the coffee at a 1:2 or 1:3 coffee-to-water ratio. Refrigerate the remaining coffee concentrate in a sealed container for up to 1 week.

Add 1 to 2 teaspoons blackstrap molasses to taste and top with the infused rum. Serve with Almond Milk and Vanilla Ice Cubes.

SUPERFOOD SPOTLIGHT

The molasses help absorb the minerals in both the molasses and the coffee, maximizing your mineral intake and aiding in the growth and development of bones.

✦ ✦ ✦ ✦

TOASTED COCONUT

The sweetness and creamy texture of this delightful concoction is created with all-natural dates and cashews.

MAKES 2 SERVINGS

¼ cup dried unsweetened shredded coconut
4 ounces bourbon
¼ cup raw cashews
1½ cups coconut water
4 Medjool dates, pitted
2 cups frozen coconut water

In a small skillet, toast the coconut over medium-high heat, stirring constantly, until golden. Transfer to a bowl and let cool. Pour the bourbon over the coconut and let soak.

Place the cashews, coconut water, and dates in a blender and blend until smooth. Add the bourbon-soaked coconut and frozen coconut water and blend until frosty.

✦ ✦ ✦ ✦

SUPERFOOD SPOTLIGHT

Delicate cashews work to lower your risk of cardiovascular and coronary heart disease, while dates are excellent for illness and injury recovery.

✦ ✦ ✦ ✦

COCOA BLAST

Rich, dreamy chocolate pops with the tartness of cherries. You're welcome.

MAKES 2 POPS

4 Medjool dates, pitted
¼ cup dried, unsweetened cherries
2 tablespoons cacao powder
1 cup coconut milk
4 ounces bourbon

Place all the ingredients, except the bourbon, in a blender and blend until creamy and smooth. Add ice and blend until frosty. Add the bourbon. Pour into two Popsicle molds, insert Popsicle sticks, and freeze for a minimum of 4 hours.

✦ ✦ ✦ ✦

SUPERFOOD SPOTLIGHT

Made with raw cacao, this frozen treat promotes detoxification and aids in the absorption of calcium.

✦ ✦ ✦ ✦

PIÑA COLADA

Upgrade the classic flavor combination of the piña colada with all fresh ingredients and none of the processed sugar.

2 ounces rum
1 cup pineapple chunks
¼ cup coconut milk

Place all the ingredients in a blender, add ½ cup of ice, and process until completely smooth.

Pour into a tall glass and sip, preferably poolside.

+ + + +

SUPERFOOD SPOTLIGHT

Let the goodness of fresh pineapple shine, knowing it is an excellent source of vitamin C and manganese; a very good source of copper; and a good source of vitamins B_1, B_5, B_6, B_9, and dietary fiber.

+ + + +

ACKNOWLEDGMENTS

I feel incredibly grateful to be surrounded by such a strong, passionate, and talented group of friends, collaborators, and loved ones, all of whom played a part in making this book a very special one.

It began with my wonderful agent, Marilyn Allen, who ever so patiently guided me through every step of the way. Thank you for believing in me and encouraging me through it all.

An enormous thank you to Gyorgy Papp for making these pages come alive with all his mouth-watering photographs. I couldn't have picked a better photographer to bring my vision to life. I had an absolute blast creating with you.

A massive thank you to everyone at Countryman Press for giving this book such a beautiful treatment. Special thanks to my talented editor, Ann Treistman, for bringing the book to life; my copy editor, Iris Bass, for your thorough and capable care; Sarah Bennett, for your unwavering patience and enthusiasm; Devon Zahn, Paul Nielsen, and Bonnie Clas for the lovely design, layout, and book cover; and to the countless others working behind the scenes—you are all much appreciated.

A huge thank you to my beautiful friends and family for the endless support and encouragement I've received throughout the years. You are forever loved.

Lastly, to the talented bartenders with whom I've had the pleasure of sharing the bar, as well as my favorite regulars—please continue to inspire me.

RESOURCES

ORGANIC LIQUORS:

4copas.com

Bluecoatgin.com

Cropvodka.com

Cucafrescaspirit.com

Greenbar.biz

Greenmountaindistillers.com

Hangarone.com

Maisonjomere.com—junipergreen,
UK5, papagayo rum

Organicnationspirits.com

Peakspirits.com

Prairievodka.com

Purusvodka.com

Rainvodka.com

Reykavodka.com

Rhumclementusa.com

Squareonevodka.com

Vodka14.com

Vodka360.com

ORGANIC LIQUEURS:

Loftliqueurs.com

OMcocktails.com

Veevlife.com

ORGANIC MIXERS:

Alteyaorganics.com—organic
rose water

Bittermens.com—organic bitters

Fever-Tree.com—organic sodas,
tonic water, ginger beer

Lilyofthedesert.com—organic
aloe vera juice

ORGANIC WINES:

organicvintners.com

theorganicwinecompany.com

COCKTAIL MIXERS:

Kombuchakamp.com—kombucha
starter kit and scobys

Purelyorganicproducts.com—
organic orange blossom honey,
rose syrup, and vinegars

Qtonic.com—organic sodas

Simplyorganicfoods.com—spices;
crystallized ginger; bourbon,
Madagascar and Tahitian
vanilla beans

TheSpicelab.com—exotic salts for
mixology

Wildhibiscus.com—syrups

BAR AND KITCHEN TOOLS:

Atthemeadow.com

Barbarianbartools.com— multipurpose bar tools

Cocktailkingdom.com

Cuisinart.com—quality blenders

Freshpreserving.com

Glassdharma.com—reusable glass drinking straws

Kegworks.com

Loveandvictory.com— personalized glassware and decanters

Masonshaker.com—mason jar cocktail shakers

Oxo.com—ice cube trays with lids

Pyrex.com

Rablabs.com—coasters and barware

Sempli.com—glassware (page 14)

Tequilabuffet.com—handcrafted tequila and martini buffets

Thebostonshaker.com

Tovolo.com—BPA-free silicone ice cube trays

Visualingual.com—seed bombs

Vitamix.com—high-speed blenders

Zoku.com—Popsicle makers and ice sphere makers

SUPERFOODS:

Frontiercoop.com—Dried herbs, seasonings, and extracts

Longevitywarehouse.com— organic superfoods and medicinal mushrooms

Mountainroseherbs.com— culinary and medicinal herbs and spices

NavitasNaturals.com—organic superfoods, such as cacao powder, chia seeds, goji berries, wheatgrass powder

Nutrex-Hawaii.com—spirulina

Sambazon.com—açai products

EDUCATIONAL RESOURCES:

Eatright.org—great organization providing information on superfoods and the ANDI chart

Forksoverknives.com—info on preventing disease by including more plant based whole foods

Thekindlife.com—natural lifestyle website

INDEX

ABOUT THE AUTHOR

JULES ARON is a NYC-based mixologist, beverage consultant, and natural lifestyle expert. As a certified health and nutrition

coach with a background in fitness, yoga, and qigong, she is deeply passionate about a healthy, wholesome lifestyle that includes delicious, nutritious foods that fuel the body, mind and spirit(s)! She believes healthy living should be fun, easy, and delicious. Join her on a spirited wellness journey and let's drink it all up!

ABOUT THE PHOTOGRAPHER

GYORGY PAPP is a commercial photographer specializing in the culinary world. The Hungarian-born artist spent the first part of

his life traveling the world before moving to Florida with his family. He is an espresso addict, a pastry chef, and a mixologist who enjoys exploring new places and making his sons smile. He still curses in Hungarian, laughs when people try to pronounce his name, and finds writing in the third person slightly awkward. www.papphoto.com